ST. PAUL
MURDER & MAYHEM

RON DE BEAULIEU

THE
History
PRESS

Published by The History Press
Charleston, SC
www.historypress.com

Front cover, top left: Library of Congress: Chronicling America; *top center*: Library of Congress Prints and Photographs Division; *top right*: Minnesota Historical Society: Minnesota Digital Newspaper Hub; *bottom*: Hennepin County Library Digital Collections
Back cover: Hennepin County Library Digital Collections.

First published 2023

Manufactured in the United States

ISBN 9781467155069

Library of Congress Control Number: 2023938347

Notice: The information in this book is true and complete to the best of our knowledge. It is offered without guarantee on the part of the author or The History Press. The author and The History Press disclaim all liability in connection with the use of this book.

CONTENTS

PREFACE

I n spite of the intense winters, it's easy to like St. Paul. It's a *nice* city. The Saintly City. It's also a (proudly) boring city,[1] but it hasn't always been that way. In its early years, the Minnesota state capital surpassed its neighbors in drinking, brawling, gambling and killing. It had a reputation for enterprise and opportunity but also for all kinds of disorder. These things coexisted in St. Paul, from its settler days through its growth into a hub of commerce.

ACKNOWLEDGEMENTS

With both this book and my previous one, *Minneapolis Murder & Mayhem*, the research would have been nearly impossible without the efficient staff at the University of Minnesota–Twin Cities libraries and the resources available through the *Chronicling America* project at the Library of Congress.

Thank you to my good friends Caitlin Cohn, Scarlett O'Donovan and Elizabeth Venditto for their careful review of the manuscript. I hope that they see how much better they have made it.

Chen-Yu Wu took all of the present-day photos in this book and was amazed at how many places St. Paul has named after a single murderer.

My writers' group offered me great encouragement during every phase of this project

John Rodrigue, the editor, has been very patient.

Rick Delaney, production editor, has done much of the work to turn this into an actual book.

I am so grateful to Conrad for napping a lot and generally being very chill, and to Calvin for working on schoolwork independently during the few days that I did the bulk of the writing. Maybe some day they will understand why I didn't let them read over my shoulder while I worked.

PART I

THE CITY GRANDFATHERS

1

THE LORDS OF THE NORTH, THE REFUGEES AND THE SCOUNDRELS

T he *Saint Paul Globe* once described Fort Snelling as "[e]ssentially a suburb of St. Paul," but St. Paul was in fact an offshoot of the fort. And it was all because the officers couldn't stop their men from sneaking out at night to get drunk in the homes of nearby civilian settlers.[2] Not only did it cause problems with their behavior (which was already bad), but it endangered them. In pursuit of alcohol in midwinter, soldiers died from drunkenly falling on the ice on the way back to the fort or getting stuck in the snow and succumbing to hypothermia. Some of their bodies were eaten by wolves. Others lost limbs from frostbite, all for a bottle of whiskey.

Finally, in 1837, a new commandant, Major Joseph Plympton, ordered the settlers to leave. "At that time, and both before and since, the commanding officers at the fort were the lords of the north. They ruled supreme[,]" an early pioneer recalled years later. "The citizens in the neighborhood of the fort were liable at any time to be thrust in the guard-house."[3] The settlers had been tilling soil and constructing permanent housing, as they believed that the land on which they lived was practically their personal property. They resisted Plympton's efforts but finally accepted that they would have to do as he ordered. They waited with bated breath for that year's round of Dakota and Ojibwe treaties, which would cede vast acreage to the United States, allowing the settlers to move over to the east bank, to what is now St. Paul, Minnesota.

Fort Snelling's round tower, rebuilt in the 1960s. *Author's collection.*

The first Dakota treaty had come in 1805, when Lieutenant Zebulon Pike signed a treaty with two Dakota leaders that granted the United States about 100,000 acres around the confluence of the Minnesota and Mississippi Rivers for a military reservation. To the Dakotas, that confluence is a sacred place, central to their creation story. Pike thought the land was worth $200,000 but did not specify this in the treaty. Congress authorized payment of only $2,000, thus commencing a long history of ripping off the Dakota nation.

No action followed on the part of the U.S. government for years. Then, in 1819, the news reached Washington, D.C., that a well-meaning Scottish nobleman, Lord Selkirk, had established a Red River settlement in modern-day Winnipeg to give displaced farmers from his homeland and Ireland a new start in Canada. Europeans of other nationalities, primarily Swiss, came as well. It was only four years since the end of the War of 1812, and U.S. officials were concerned by the presence of a British settlement in such proximity to the border. This was a potential security risk and threatened U.S. trade dominance in the region: British traders had opened a post within U.S. territory, and were selling goods from the Selkirkers to the Natives in exchange for pelts.

"Fort Snelling from Across the River." *Hennepin County Library Digital Collections*.

Watchtower at Fort Snelling. *Hennepin County Library Digital Collections*.

"Promontory and Lookout at Fort Snelling." *Hennepin County Library Digital Collections.*

In the mid-1820s, the Selkirk settlement endured violent harassment from nearby fur traders, was beset by grasshoppers and thwarted by harsh winters and floods. The commandant of Fort Snelling, Colonel Josiah Snelling himself, gave indications that the Selkirkers were welcome to stay on the reservation. In 1827, a wave of refugees relocated to the land just to the west of the fort. Some became soldiers or civilian employees of the fort. Others had no direct connection to the military at all, and this population grew to 157 over the next ten years as discharged soldiers joined the community. In addition to mundane occupations such as cattle-raising, and illicit whiskey sales, a fair number of them joined the fur trade.

This clique was so destructive that the Indian agent Lawrence Taliaferro brought the Dakota chiefs to Washington, D.C., for the 1837 treaty negotiations specifically to get them away from the traders; not that he succeeded. Some of the traders had the resources to make their way to the capital. Earlier in the year, at a treaty council involving the Ojibwes, a trader had used his influence to get a line entered in the treaty that would have provided him with $20,000 to be paid by the Ojibwes, despite the fact that they did not owe it to him. Taliaferro pulled a gun on the instigator, to the consternation of Commissioner Henry Dodge, but "much to the chagrin of the sensible thinking Indians and surprise of intelligent lookers-on," the line remained in the treaty.[4]

Taliaferro had arrived at the military reservation in July 1820 at the age of twenty-six. He had distinguished himself in the War of 1812, having enlisted at eighteen after being educated at home on the Whitehall Plantation in King George County, Virginia. He got the job of Indian agent because he paid President James Monroe a social call back in 1818, and the president took a shine to him.

Predictably, for a person of Taliaferro's social position as the son of a wealthy plantation owner, he proved to be egotistical, bordering on delusional, and was blissfully unaware of his own faults. He was also honest in his dealings and happy to make enemies with anyone who opposed his goals. As traders set up posts near the fort, he attempted to prevent them from defrauding the Dakotas, Ojibwes and other Natives who came there to exchange furs for goods. Taliaferro had the power to grant and suspend traders' licenses for misconduct. He exercised that power as liberally as he could and washed his hands of responsibility when the traders' "clients" assaulted them in frustration. There were initially only two trading posts, and he refused to increase the number. Secretary of War John C. Calhoun ordered him to reverse this policy; by 1826, there were thirteen posts.

Like many Euro-Americans looking to establish relationships with Natives, Taliaferro married a Native woman, The Day Sets, and had a child with her. His father-in-law, the Bde Maka Ska chief Man of the Sky (also called "Cloud Man") loved him, but many Dakotas resented Taliaferro. He treated them like children and even *called* them his children. He was grandiose and frank, his un-self-aware puffery matching the inflamed rhetoric that Native political leaders deliberately inserted into their own speechmaking. This made Taliaferro, on the surface, a good fit for the role. The Dakotas knew that they could trust him to tell them what he really thought. The trouble was that he was sometimes badly wrong and arrogant in the conviction of his rightness.

He did have a point about the traders, though. It was a centuries-old tradition by that time for fur traders to unscrupulously trap Natives in a debt cycle. Traders would provide goods on credit, and Natives would pay them back in pelts at the end of the hunting season, at the value of 200 percent or more of the value of the initial purchase. It was impossible for them to avoid doing business with the traders, who were their main source for metal goods, including the guns they needed for both hunting game and self-defense. The Dakotas were locked in what seemed like an interminable war with Ojibwes, as the latter nation was shoved west by their eastern enemies, the Iroquois. Population increase as a result of that, along with American settler colonization, further shrank available space for hunting grounds and depleted a food supply that was already hurting from overhunting for pelts to trade.

Taliaferro initially believed that Henry H. Sibley, the first practicing attorney in the region, was the least bad of the traders. This could have been class prejudice: Sibley, unlike most fur traders, came from a respectable family. His father was a U.S. Attorney who had served in Congress and had been a commissioner in Indian treaty negotiations in Illinois and Michigan. In 1834, Henry came to the American Fur Company's trading post in Mendota, across the Minnesota River from the military reservation. He had a gift for political stratagems that would make him more dangerous to Taliaferro's agenda than a garden-variety trader ever could be.

President Zachary Taylor had once remarked in a letter to the agent that the American Fur Company was "the [damned] greatest [set of] scoundrels the world ever knew," and Taliaferro agreed.[5] The treaties of that year, 1837, marked a point at which trading companies pivoted from profiting from fur sales (the declining game population and encroaching settlers made this a waning enterprise) to profiting from treaty negotiations.[6] The traders, Sibley among them, began to leverage political connections on the one hand while exploiting their friendships with Native signatories on the other to manipulate or trick them into accepting unfair terms and then exerting their influence to ensure that traders, not Natives, were first to be paid from the annuities.

At the Dakotas' 1837 treaty council in D.C., a few traders, including Sibley, secured a guarantee in the treaty of $90,000 for themselves. The Native signatories had been reluctant to give up their land, but they trusted Taliaferro, who in turn trusted the U.S. government and the treaty process. He had no understanding of political machinations. When he had started out as a new Indian agent, he had been "a child in such matters" who "believed himself honest in all things; deeming every other man whatever his station equally so."[7] After nearly twenty years of failing to prevent abuse by the traders, "the human heart seemed [to him] deceitful above all things and desperately wicked."[8]

NO JUSTICE FOR JOHN HAYS

Across from Fort Snelling, settlers immediately began to stake claims. By law, a land claimant needed only to build a living structure and mark the area around it as their own. A "claim" was not "ownership," but it could become so. Within a few years' time, a claimant could expect Uncle Sam to come knocking. The claimant would have to pay up, but very little, only a fraction of the value of the land.

Active members of the military were not allowed to take advantage of the location of their postings to snap up this prime real estate. Some high-ranking officers went right ahead and staked claims and then relied on their position to discourage anyone from giving them a hard time about it. Others, of lower rank, resorted to bribery; still others crossed their fingers and prayed that the indifference of their superiors would allow their illegal claim to go unnoticed.

Private Edward Phelan, from Londonderry, Ireland, didn't need to bend the rules. He was discharged from the army on June 8, 1838, which was just in time for the treaty ratification. He chose a riverside tract "running back to the bluff, and bounded (approximately) by what is now Eagle and Third streets [that stretch of Third Street is now Kellogg Boulevard] on the west, and Saint Peter street on the east."[9]

Sergeant John Hays, Phelan's fellow Irishman, had had his term of service extended, and he wouldn't get out until the spring of 1839. He was eager to claim land, but he was also an honest man. The only untruth that has ever been attributed to him was his age: according to his military record, he was forty years old at the time of his discharge, but he appeared to be far older, meaning that he might have lied about how old he was in order to join the military after coming to the United States from Ireland.

Hays had served in the U.S. Army for about a decade. During that time, he impressed all who knew him with both his strict discipline and unwavering kindness. He would never have dreamed of resorting to illegal measures to turn a profit. Instead, he approached Phelan and suggested that they team up. Phelan was everything that Hays was not: Phelan was impulsive, vicious and dishonest. He was younger than Hays, to be sure, but at twenty-eight years old, youth alone could not explain his poor conduct. He was believed to be dangerous and had a history of violence. His acquaintances remembered him as "immoral, cruel, [and] revengeful."[10] He was six foot, two inches tall, five inches taller than Hays, and well-built, and he liked to use his strength to his advantage against smaller men. In sum, he was a compulsive bully.

Hays instructed Phelan to stake out a claim next to his own. Hays, who was a childless bachelor, had accumulated savings. He gave some of it to Phelan to buy the building materials for a cabin that they could live in together once Hays was discharged. Phelan did what Hays told him to do. He chose a riverside tract abutting his own on the east, "running back to the bluffs, extending probably from what is now Saint Peter street, down to somewhere near the present Minnesota street."[11] He built the cabin tucked into the bluff's side.

Phelan had not been on the east bank long before he stole a pig from James Thompson, a freedman who lived in nearby Kaposia, the west bank village of the chief Big Thunder (often called "Little Crow" or "Petit Corbeau" by non-Natives, as were his father, grandfather and son). Thompson didn't want any trouble. He waited until Phelan wandered briefly from his cabin and then snuck his pig back. Phelan confronted him, physically fought him for the pig, and lost.

When Hays joined Phelan on April 25, 1839, the older man fit in well in the community, where he was universally liked. Regardless, he and Phelan rarely had visitors. Phelan "was regarded by the other settlers as a bad, unscrupulous, wicked man."[12] Hays may have been good-natured, but he didn't get along with Phelan. Still, they cooperated well enough to keep things running and jointly owned some assets, including cattle.

Hays saw a light at the end of the tunnel: he did not intend for this to be a permanent arrangement. He told his army buddy Bartholomew Baldwin that he planned to marry a Native woman.[13] He kept his life savings, $200,

Riverfront view of the approximate area where Phelan and Hays's claims once rested. *Author's collection.*

away from home, in the care of his friend Lieutenant Daniel McPhail, out of Phelan's reach.

At 9:00 p.m. on Thursday, September 5, 1839, former soldier William Evans was at home entertaining his neighbors, the lumbermen Stephen Scott and John Foy. Phelan, who lived about one and a half miles upriver, appeared, wearing mud-soaked clothes. His head was bare, as he had lost his hat, and he carried a canoe paddle. Phelan explained that he had fallen off a log as he was crossing a creek while searching for a calf that he had lost. Evans told the bedraggled man to spend the night at his cabin. The next morning, Phelan told Evans that he would head back home, looking for the calf along the way, and that if he couldn't find it, Hays would go to Kaposia to look for it. Evans, Foy and Scott left after breakfast, before Phelan went out.

Later that morning, on the river, Scott saw Phelan depart in his canoe from Phelan's Landing, a stretch of riverbank on his claim that was later developed into the Upper Levee. Foy saw him, too. The English fur trader James R. Clewett was out on a boat that day and also saw Phelan, as did his business partners Henry C. Mencke and Joseph R. Brown, the latter of

whom was the east bank justice of the peace and owned a thriving saloon on Grey Cloud Island. All five men saw that Phelan stayed along the east bank, without crossing the river as he would have had to do if he were going to Kaposia. They took their eyes off him just long enough for Scott and Foy to buy whiskey from Mencke at his shack, and then Scott and Foy resumed their journey and had Phelan in sight once more, still along the east bank. The lapse in time when they weren't watching was not enough for him to have gone over to the other side and then come back.

Around 8:30 that morning, Scott and Foy got out of their canoes at Phelan's Landing. Foy trotted up the bluff to Phelan's cabin, but Scott meandered a little, exploring a trail along the river bottom.[14] After about seventy-five yards, the trail ended. Scott saw that the grass had been flattened. There was a large pool of fresh blood, and drops of it were scattered around on the grass. He thought it looked like some heavy creature had been lying on the flattened grass, and he assumed that a Native had injured a cow, as they sometimes shot at them, but on the other hand he did not think that a cow would have any reason to be there.

Scott went on to Phelan's cabin, and Phelan said that he had just come back across the river after dropping Hays off so that he could search for the calf in Kaposia. Scott asked him if they had an injured cow, but Phelan said that they did not and suggested that one of their neighbors, the Gervais family, might have one. He casually changed the subject and told his visitors about a disagreement he'd been having with Hays. They were building a root house and were digging clay out of the hill to make room for it. Hays wanted to chuck the clay farther up the hill, while Phelan wanted to move it farther down. Scott and Foy didn't stay long, and they left around 9:00 a.m.

That evening, Mrs. Genevieve Gervais was at home in her cabin, recovering from giving birth two days earlier to Basil Gervais, the first single-race white child born in future St. Paul. Phelan showed up and tried to tell her something, but she was hard of hearing. She understood enough to know that Phelan hadn't come to congratulate her but instead to tell her that an "Indian" had stolen a calf, and so Hays had gone across the river to Kaposia.

Two days later, on Sunday, September 8, Phelan returned to see the Gervais family. He told them that Hays had disappeared, but that he had told Phelan that he might go to Grey Cloud Island to visit the fur trader Hazen P. Mooers, which could explain why he had been gone for so long.

Mrs. Gervais suggested that Phelan go to see her friend and neighbor Abraham Perry, a Swiss watchmaker who now worked at farming and cattle-raising. Joseph R. Brown had come from Grey Cloud Island to visit the Perrys, and he would know if Hays had been there. Phelan replied that he wouldn't go to see Perry, because he wasn't dressed well enough for it, although he apparently was dressed well enough to visit the Gervais family. Before leaving, Phelan also told them that the calf had come back of its own accord.

The next day, Monday the ninth, Ben Gervais, Genevieve's husband, went out to search for Hays. He and Phelan started at Phelan's Landing and proceeded all the way to Kaposia. Phelan inquired at the mission house if they had seen Hays but was told that he hadn't been to the village. Gervais and Phelan then scoured the river bottoms, but Hays wasn't there, either.

It wasn't until two days later, on Wednesday, that Phelan went to Fort Snelling, "where Hays was well known and liked."[15] As one of Hays's good friends, Baldwin was the first person whom Phelan and Gervais involved in the search. He joined them, treading the same ground that they had, even going to Kaposia himself to look for Hays. Phelan said that "Indians" had probably killed Hays, and he gave up the search. According to Phelan, two months before Hays's disappearance, an Indian youth had fired a gun into their home, and Hays had threatened to beat him if he did it again. The boy left, but not before threatening Hays in return.

Interior of Wakan Tipi cave, 1870. *Hennepin County Library Digital Collections.*

By September 15, the rumor had grown: Big Thunder himself was said to have murdered Hays. Taliaferro discarded the notion out of hand. He wrote in his journal, "No belief rests in me [that Big Thunder killed him]." The agent had his own suspicions about the reason for Hays's disappearance: "His neighbor, Phelan, knows something. Hays lived with him and had money."[16]

Exactly two weeks later, on September 29, a Dakota man, Dancer, came to see Taliaferro. Dancer said that his children had found John Hays's body in the river by Wakan Tipi, which the settlers and soldiers called "Carver's Cave." Taliaferro informed Plympton, who arranged a search party and sent them out the next day. Lieutenant McPhail was in charge. Along with

"Looking Out of [Wakan Tipi cave] Towards St. Paul," 1875. *Hennepin County Library Digital Collections.*

him came Dancer; the fort surgeon, Dr. John Emerson; the sutler, Franklin Steele; and Baldwin. Dancer remarked that the body wasn't exactly where his children had found it; it was slightly downriver of where he had thought it would be.

It had been a very cold, dry September, at times below freezing. Decomposition had been stalled enough for Hays to be identifiable. His corpse, which had been stripped naked, lay face-up on the riverbank with his legs in the water. He was covered in grass and sand. Emerson had the body washed and then saw that "his head, jaws, and nose were…badly mashed by violent blows, unmistakably indicating a desperate murder."[17] Emerson said later that the weapon could have been a canoe paddle.

After they buried Hays near the spot where they found him, Baldwin walked along the riverbank, toward the place where Dancer had expected to find the body. It was in the vicinity of Phelan's claim.[18] Baldwin found a trail created by trampled greenery and grass. He saw gray hairs in the grass and assumed they were wolf hairs. They looked longer than Hays's hair.

WITHIN THE NEXT FEW days, Henry H. Sibley, who was the west bank justice of the peace, interviewed Phelan. Phelan told him that he and Hays had gotten along well but that he didn't know anything about Hays's finances. Phelan also said that when Hays went to Kaposia, he wasn't looking for a confrontation, only to learn what had become of the calf.

At that time, the burgeoning east bank settlement fell into the sprawling Wisconsin Territory. To stand trial, Phelan would have to be taken to Prairie du Chien, a nearly two-hundred-mile-long journey southeast via the Mississippi River. Although Sibley had handled the preliminaries, the investigation was handed over to Brown, who issued an arrest warrant for Phelan on October 31. Baldwin sat for a deposition, during which he told Brown that he had no reason to suspect that Phelan had murdered Hays. Brown reinterviewed Phelan, along with the neighbors: Evans, in whose home Phelan had slept on the night of September 5; Foy and Scott, who had visited Phelan on the morning of September 6; and the Gervais family. Mr. Gervais and one of his sons, fourteen-year-old Alphonse, told Brown that their cattle did roam the river bottom below Phelan's cabin, but none of them had been hurt, which meant that an injured cow could not explain the pool of blood that Scott had seen on the morning of the sixth. Gervais also said that they would have found out if one of their neighbors' cattle had been injured, but they knew of no such thing.

The grass and sand that Emerson had ordered to be washed off of Hays's body had not been there when Dancer's kids originally found the body. Phelan told Brown that he had received word of the discovery of the body on September 29, the same day as Taliaferro. It had been too late in the day for Phelan to go view it, so he went the next morning. He said that he had found Hays's corpse on the riverbank submerged in water up to the shoulders. Phelan hauled him

Henry H. Sibley. *Library of Congress: Chronicling America.*

mostly out of the water and covered him with the debris that the search party had observed.

Phelan did not make a favorable impression on Brown. He contradicted and disputed the testimony of his neighbors, but their recollections validated one another's, casting doubt on his story, not theirs. Scott and Foy said Phelan had told them that he had crossed the river before their visit to his cabin on Friday, September 6. Now Phelan told Brown that he had rowed Hays across the river *after* Scott and Foy left his cabin that morning.

Brown weighed the facts he had learned from the neighbors and compared it to what Phelan had told him and concluded that: (1) Phelan couldn't have crossed the river that morning, as he had told Scott and Foy, because they and the other three men (including Brown) on the river would have seen him; and (2) when Scott told him about the blood at the river bottom and asked if he had an injured cow, Phelan didn't consider it a possibility. Brown wrote in his casebook, "[if] he really had a calf lost the circumstances of the blood in the bottom would have convinced him that it was the blood of his calf." Brown considered "the affair of the [stolen] calf a fabrication."[19] He deduced that Phelan's reason for telling the Gervais family and, later, Baldwin that Hays had gone to Grey Cloud Island was to throw them off the scent. Finally, Brown believed that, on the night of Thursday, September 5, when Phelan first kicked off the Hays drama by wandering into Evans's house covered in mud, he had just come from murdering Hays. Otherwise, Brown mused, "what was he doing with a canoe paddle when searching for a calf on land?"[20] If Brown was correct, then the first white person's birth (Basil Gervais's) preceded the first white person's death (Hays's) by one day.

Brown charged Phelan with murder in the first degree and had him jailed in the Fort Snelling guardhouse to await the arrival of the next steamboat to Prairie du Chien. By that time of year, November, weather conditions and ice prevented steamboat traffic, so Phelan was incarcerated for about six months. In the spring of 1840, he was brought to Prairie du Chien. Mr. Evans and Mrs. Gervais were subpoenaed and had to go as well.

What happened there is lost to the sands of time.[21] What we do know is that Phelan returned to the east bank in the early summer of 1840. He found that

The following six images are a sample of locations in St. Paul named after its first murderer. Phalen Drive street sign. *Author's collection.*

Phalen Park Golf Course in winter. *Author's collection.*

Phalen Park Golf Course in winter. *Author's collection.*

another man, Vetal Guerin, had jumped (that is, "stolen") Hays's claim. If a claimant were absent for six months, then he forfeited his claim by default. Phelan went to Guerin's cabin with Clewett to translate, as Guerin did not at that time speak English. Guerin refused Phelan's demand that he leave. Phelan later came at Guerin with an axe, but Guerin had large friends who in turn threatened to throw Phelan off the bluff if he didn't walk away. Phelan backed off and filed a lawsuit against him with Joseph R. Brown, and the case went on for a year before Phelan gave up.

There were so few men in the area that Phelan was elected to represent his neighborhood at the 1848 Territorial Convention, which was conducted by the two people who had investigated his crime, Sibley and Brown (it had been Brown's idea to name this place "Minnesota," after the river). There, Phelan signed his name as "Phalen," a spelling that would be attached to more than thirty sites in present-day St. Paul.[22]

He remained a blackguard. In spring 1850, Phelan was indicted for perjury by the first grand jury convened in Ramsey County. He fled the charge and joined a westbound wagon train. Phelan was so violent toward the other men that they killed him in self-defense.

With the exception of a few people who believed that a Dakota man had committed the murder, "of Phelan's guilt no one who was resident in this vicinity had doubt." That was the conclusion the journalist J. Fletcher Williams reached. In preparation for his 1876 book, *A History of the City of Saint Paul, and of the County of Ramsey, Minnesota*, he spoke with Sibley, who said that the evidence "was such as to leave no doubt of [Phelan]'s guilt." Williams also interviewed the witnesses. Clewett, despite being among those whose testimony demonstrated that Phelan had lied when he said that he crossed the river, told Williams that he had thought an Indian killed Hays. Williams learned from him that "a few years afterward, just after [Hays's] death, [a Dakota man] confessed that he was the murderer of Hays; also, that some of the Kaposia Indians used to assert that a brother of [Big Thunder] had committed the act." Sibley told Williams that this was "impossible," explaining that he would have heard about it if a Native had committed the murder. He had had so many friends among them that it would not have been a secret from him. Just as important, "there was no particular motive for the Indians to have murdered Hays, more than any one [*sic*] else, while two powerful motives would seem to have influenced Phelan—revenge and avarice."[23]

Mrs. Gervais told Williams that sometime in the summer of 1839, not long before the murder, she had asked Phelan how things were going

Phalen Regional Park. *Author's collection.*

Phalen Regional Park. *Author's collection.*

Phalen Creek is now underground, but Hamm's Brewery, a famous local landmark, stands alongside it. *Author's collection.*

with Hays, and he replied "very badly" and added that Hays was "a lazy good-for-nothing." That sounds like Phelan projecting his weaknesses as a housemate, perhaps repeating an insult that Hays had lobbed at him. "But never mind." Phelan continued, "I'll soon be rid of him." Williams reported a grisly tale from Alphonse Gervais, who, at the time of the interview, was a middle-aged man: he had seen Phelan wearing bloody clothes. Also, when the investigators searched the cabin, they had found bloody clothes hidden there. That could have been either Phelan's clothing or Hays's, as Hays's corpse had been found naked. Or it could have been both men's clothing. Alphonse's dog, following a scent, led the way to a pool of blood, probably the same one that Scott had observed, and the dog proceeded to follow the trail "by which the body was dragged to the river from thence."[24]

Williams summarized the case in this way: "There is, then, no alternative left, but to record PHELAN as the murderer of HAYS. He must stand, on the chronicles of our city, as its CAIN—the first who imbrued his hands with the blood of his brother—a crime too often, alas, repeated since that day."[25]

3
UNSETTLING SETTLEMENT

Guerin moving into Hays's claim wasn't the only change that Phelan found when he returned to the east bank. Many of his neighbors' cabins had been destroyed by Fort Snelling soldiers. The fault lay with both fur traders and whiskey sellers. Prominent among the latter was Pierre "Pig's Eye" Parrant, a notorious saloonkeeper from Canada.

Agent Taliaferro had issued an order prohibiting Parrant from participating in the liquor trade and from entering Indian country. Believing himself to be complying with the prohibition without losing his customer base of soldiers and Natives, Parrant set up a whiskey shack at the mouth of the creek flowing from Fountain Cave around the same time as Phelan settled on the east bank, in June 1838. Abraham Perry also crossed the river that month but for a different reason from Parrant's: he wanted a permanent home for his family.

The Dakotas had not yet received their treaty annuity payment and were angry that the settlers were on their land before they had been paid for it. Some of them killed the Perry family's cattle. Taliaferro took Perry's side and made the Dakotas reimburse him for the loss. Major Plympton cleared the west bank of settlers, and Perry, Parrant and Phelan quickly had company.

Parrant continued to cause difficulties for the Fort Snelling authorities. Soldiers were crossing the river to his shanty, getting drunk and not showing up the next day. The guards at the fort would come find them and throw them in the guardhouse.

Parrant's operation was not, of course, the only whiskey game in town. The east bank settlement, which would soon be dubbed "Pig's Eye Landing"

"Fountain Cave." *Hennepin County Library Digital Collections.*

in his honor, was before that known as "Rumtown." On April 14, 1839, the *Ariel*, the first steamboat of the season, arrived, bringing twenty whiskey barrels for Joseph R. Brown. On June 3, a large party of soldiers came to Mencke's shop. That night, forty-seven of them were held in the guardhouse for drunkenness. Mencke was among Taliaferro's most-hated settlers for the high volume of whiskey he also sold to Natives.

On April 23, 1839, Dr. Emerson[26] wrote a dramatic letter to the surgeon general.

> *Since the middle of winter we have been completely inundated with ardent spirits, and consequently the most beastly scenes of intoxication among the soldiers of this garrison and the Indians in its vicinity, which, no doubt, will add many cases to our sick-list. The whisky is brought here by citizens*

*who are pouring in upon us and settling themselves on the opposite shore of
the Mississippi River in defiance of our worthy commanding officer, Major
J. Plympton, whose authority they set at naught.*[27]

The surgeon general, having read Emerson's letter, wrote to the secretary
of war, "The immediate action of the Government is called for in this
matter."[28]

On June 2, Brigadier General John E. Wool arrived to inspect the military
post. He walked away from his investigation agreeing with Plympton, but he
had a different main concern: "The white inhabitants [of the settlement],
aware of the large amount of money annually paid by the United States
to the Indians [from treaty annuities], avail themselves of the means in
their power…of introducing…intoxicating liquors." He acknowledged
that this was "destructive to the discipline of the troops"; moreover, it was
"hazardous of the peace and quiet of the country." He did not want liquor
"introduced into the Indian country" at all. Wool went on: "It is well known
that the [Dakota] Sioux and Chippewas [Ojibwes] have been at war….
The introduction of whisky, which is as common almost as water…prompts
collision and war."[29] He agreed that the settlers had to go. "Such is the
character of the white inhabitants of that country, that if they cannot be
permitted to carry on their nefarious traffic with the Indians, it will sooner
or later involve them in a war with the United States."[30]

By that time, Taliaferro had grown weary, disenchanted and sickly. He
wrote to the War Department, resigning his position. Sibley and some other
traders from the American Fur Company requested a meeting with him.
There, on the basis of a false statement from one of the traders, Philander
Prescott, they accused Taliaferro of "authorizing" a Dakota man, Bad Hail,
to destroy Mencke's saloon and set fire to his home. Taliaferro was stunned.
Bad Hail had come to him some months earlier and had asked for the agent's
permission to drive the settlers away from the east bank until the annuity
payment arrived. Taliaferro had replied that neither he nor Bad Hail and
his fellow Dakotas "had any business with these bad men." Not long after
that meeting between Taliaferro and the traders, Clewett somehow obtained
a writ from the sheriff of Clayton County, Iowa, and deputized Mencke
to arrest the Indian agent. Mencke found Taliaferro in the Fort Snelling
infirmary. Mencke threw the patient to the floor, knelt on his stomach and
put a pistol to his ear. A canoe was waiting, said Mencke, and they were
leaving now, bound for Clayton Court House, just as Phelan had been taken
to Prairie du Chien for trial. "Put up your pistol, Mr. Menck[e], or whatever

your name is," Taliaferro replied "coolly." He did not resist, but said, "I wish only time to send a note to the Fort previous to leaving." Mencke allowed him to do this, and Plympton's guards came to Taliaferro's rescue. The Indian agent now had a score to settle. He attempted to withdraw his resignation, but his request was denied. His involvement in the region came to an end. It is practically a refrain among chroniclers of Minnesota history that Taliaferro was the last honest agent the Dakotas ever had.

Major Plympton had had enough. He managed to scare Mencke into leaving and never coming back, but he wanted the other east bank settlers pushed farther away from Fort Snelling as well. He sent his map to the War Department on October 5, along with an explanatory note. "The limits of the Reservation, as now marked, embrace no more ground...than is absolutely necessary to furnish the daily wants of this garrison."[31] According to Williams, "The limits fixed were entirely arbitrary. They were *not* governed by the 'daily wants' of the garrison....The line was extended far beyond the possible intent of the Reservation (emphasis in original)."[32] It ran right across the river, over a large section of present-day St. Paul, reaching as far east as Seven Corners.

About two weeks later, Joel R. Poinsett, the secretary of war, ordered "that the intruders on the land recently reserved for military purposes, opposite to that post east of the Mississippi River, be removed." His order authorized the use of force.[33] The settlers appealed to civilian authorities, who sided with them, but the war department had more power, and on May 6, 1840, "the soldiery fell upon [the settlers] without warning, treated them with unjustifiable rudeness, broke and destroyed furniture wantonly, insulted the women, and, in one or two instances, fired at and killed cattle."[34] The settlers moved just beyond Plympton's boundary, where a few families, fur traders and former soldiers were already putting down roots.

Following the ratification of the 1837 treaties, the United States conducted surveys of the land, in preparation for further settlement, which was beginning to snowball. In 1841, the little east bank community took the name "St. Paul." New stores opened, but at that time most of their customers were Natives. Traders were transitioning away from accepting furs as payment. For one thing, the fauna were too depleted, for another, silk was overtaking fur in European clothing fashions, and, most importantly, annuity payments put cash in the hands of Natives that they could exchange instead. Throughout the 1840s, these payments were the primary cash supply all along the Minnesota and Mississippi Rivers. [35]

Auguste L. Larpenteur, who arrived in 1843 at the age of twenty to work at a trader's store, later recalled that St. Paul at that time was "nothing but an Indian community."[36] They lived elsewhere, but came into town by the hundreds to conduct their business. Larpenteur was impressed with how well they conserved their scarce resources, with their trustworthiness and with the good behavior of their children. They considered him a friend and named him Wam-dus-ka ("The Serpent").

It was not all smooth sailing for the young store clerk. One evening, a Native man came to his house and, after Larpenteur attempted to show him polite hospitality, attacked his host with a knife. Larpenteur beat him to a pulp and hurled him over the bluff. The next morning, the man came crawling back. Larpenteur helped him to clean his wounds, and the two became friends.

Auguste L. Larpenteur.
Minnesota Historical Society:
Minnesota Digital Newspaper Hub.

The Guerin family had similar encounters. On January 26, 1841, Vetal Guerin married Adele Perry, a child of fourteen, and brought her to live with him on Hays's old claim. It was an ill-omened spot, or so it must have seemed. They lived close to the whiskey shop that Parrant had built farther from the fort after being forced to move from his old location within Plympton's boundary. The Natives who came to drink there passed by the Guerin claim on their way back to their camp, killing livestock and committing vandalism. This pattern continued for years. One time, a Native friend came to visit, but she was drunk, and so the Guerins did not let her come inside. She broke a window with a stick. Mr. Guerin came out of the house, picked her up and carried her to the edge of his yard. The woman screamed at him, and some more Natives came running. They, too, were drunk. Mr. Guerin ran back into his house, where Mrs. Guerin was nursing their infant son. Two arrows flew inside before Mr. Guerin closed the door. Their attackers tried to enter through the broken window.

Mrs. Guerin hid under the bed with her baby, expecting to be killed. Mr. Guerin wielded an axe to defend himself and his family, but in came the chief Hawk's Bill, sober and sensible. He sent the Guerins next door to stay with Ben Gervais, to whom Mr. Guerin had donated half of the claim after the Gervais family was driven off of their old claim by the soldiers. Hawk's Bill got the mob to leave, but not before they had killed the Guerins' dog. A few of them returned in the evening and fired barbed arrows at the family's cattle. Mr. Guerin himself was shot at multiple times after that night, but none of the bullets struck him.

And then there was the Gammel family, whose home on Pig's Eye Lake became the site of a battle. One summer morning in 1842, Francis Gammel and his wife, a Dakota woman, were hoeing corn with the help of Rattler, a Dakota man, and one of Rattler's wives. Rattler's other wife wasn't feeling well, and she had gone into the house. Rattler followed after her. Three children, Rattler's son and daughter and the infant David Gammel, were with the three adults remaining in the field. An advance party of Ojibwes intent on attacking Kaposia was sneaking through the brush by a creek that drained into the lake. They recognized Mrs. Gammel and Rattler's wife as Dakotas and shot at them. Rattler's wife died in her tracks. Mrs. Gammel was badly hurt. Mr. Gammel lifted her and brought her into the house. The Ojibwes pursued them indoors and scalped Mrs. Gammel as she lay dying in her husband's arms. They ran off, shouting to announce that they had taken a scalp. Mr. Gammel set down his wife, picked up his gun and fired. He hit an Ojibwe man in the leg. All of those warriors got away, but not before cutting off the head of Rattler's little boy.

That shout saved the lives of the Dakotas of Kaposia. The Ojibwe reconnoiterers had blown the cover for their whole war party. They could have bowled over the Kaposians if they had kept quiet and attacked them unawares: the men of Kaposia were on a collective whiskey spree, meaning that the women had hidden their weapons. As it was, the men had time to get to their firearms and to cross the river and attack.

Incessant firing and hand-to-hand combat lasted for several hours. Around noon, the Ojibwes began to retreat. The Dakotas chased them over the bluff and several miles beyond that. Nine or ten Ojibwe corpses lay in the Gammel cornfield. The Dakotas lost twice as many warriors. Their survivors among the men scalped the fallen enemies, while the women hacked at the corpses. Rattler's sister Berry Picker, known to the settlers as "Old Bets," bashed their heads with a club. She had a special grievance: in addition to the loss of her brother's wife, her own son was wounded in the battle.

This became known as the "Battle of Kaposia," and it is from this event that Battle Creek, along which the Ojibwe warriors approached the

Gammel farm, got its name. Would there have been fewer Dakota losses if the men had been sober? Would there have been a battle at all without the liquid courage that often fueled these incidents?

Auguste Larpenteur acknowledged years later that "you hear frightful stories of [the Natives'] devotion to firewater, but there were no more drunkards among [them] at that time than there were among the white men."[37] Alcohol was a problem for the whole area. Whiskey made "brutes of the white men" and St. Paul "a by-word."[38]

PERHAPS THEY DIDN'T EVEN need whiskey. The first land sales were held at the St. Croix Falls land office that same year. Sibley had been appointed representative of the east bank settlers to buy the land on their behalf. It was an auction, and St. Paulites feared that out-of-town speculators would outbid them. Therefore, and to Sibley's surprise, he was accompanied and surrounded by large, armed men, the implication being that they would thrash anyone who bid against him. No other community felt the need to do this, and it was thoroughly unnecessary. St. Paulites were primed for violence. The years to come would make that all too clear.

PART II

GROWING PAINS

4
FATAL NEWS

James M. Goodhue had a bachelor's degree in geology from Amherst College. This had the potential to lead to a lucrative career, as he was living in an era of U.S. westward expansion and resource exploration, but Goodhue was not guided by the pursuit of wealth. He went into law instead, then became a newsman when he stepped in as a temporary editor for a Wisconsin newspaper after the editor quit.

In 1849, St. Paul was poised to explode in population. It was the largest settlement in the newly minted Minnesota Territory. While it was accessible only by river, the in-progress Territorial Road would soon connect it to Hudson, Wisconsin. The little town on the Mississippi was about to attract enterprising Easterners like honey draws flies. Goodhue, age thirty-nine, was among the first. He stepped off the boat on a "'raw, cloudy day'" in mid-April. The weather remained ominous, "cold and stormy."[39] When he arrived, St. Paul consisted of a mere thirty buildings.

Goodhue had shipped a press and type to the city first and then followed his machinery. He had planned to call his paper the *Epistle of Saint Paul*, but his friends persuaded him that this biblical reference was irreverent, and so he called it the *Minnesota Pioneer*. The original name would have matched his intentions perfectly. The *Pioneer*, he later said, "advocated Minnesota, morality, and religion from the beginning."[40]

Despite the weather, Goodhue was pleased with his new home. In the very first issue of his paper, April 28, he wrote, "A more beautiful site for a town cannot be imagined." He was as impressed with the rate of change

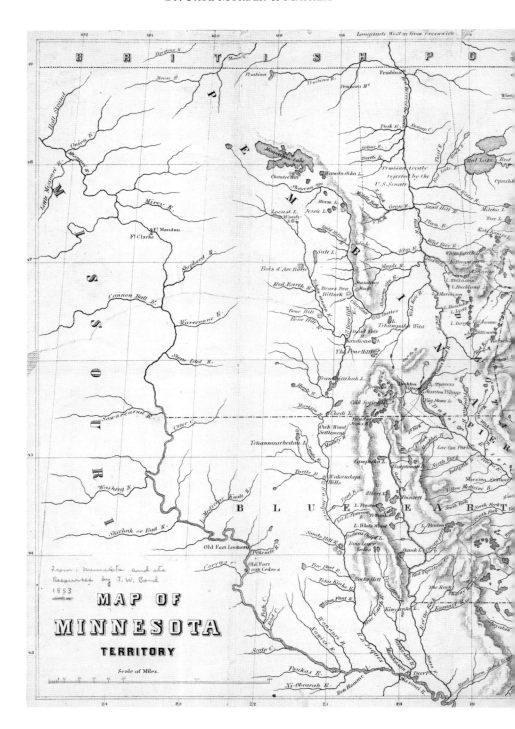

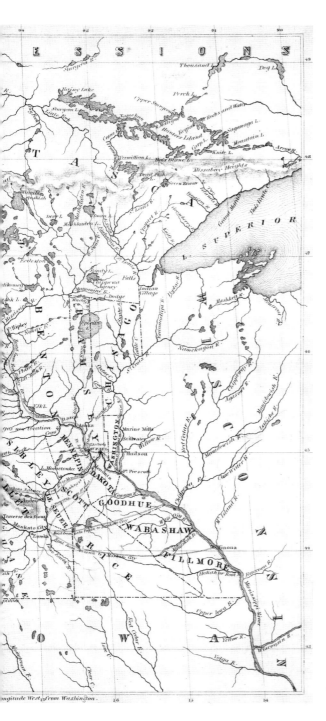

Map of the Minnesota Territory.
Hennepin County Library Digital Collections.

as he was with the natural beauty. "A description of the village now would not answer for a month hence—which is the rapidity of building....Piles of lumber and building materials lie scattered everywhere in admirable confusion...[S]tores, hotels, houses, are projected and built in a few days."[41] His descriptions of St. Paul were so enticing that he is credited with spurring migration from the East, and Goodhue County is named after him. He was a proud promoter, extolling the virtues of St. Paul's particular location: "Saint Paul, at the head of river communication, must necessarily supply the trade of all the vast regions north of it...and west to the Rocky Mountains, and east to the basin of the great Lakes, and is destined to be the focus of an immense business," as it would grow along with all of those other regions to meet their need for commerce.[42] His brother Isaac joined him in St. Paul, and together they operated a ferryboat. James built a house on the corner of Third and St. Peter Streets, where he lived with his wife and children. A population boom, which James had foreseen, came that summer, and the 1850 census enumerated 840 souls in St. Paul.[43]

He was sarcastic and courageous, traits evident in his writing. St. Paulites were not interested in politics in those days, according to Goodhue, and so his paper "gave them none."[44] This did not prevent him from commenting on the actions of politicians, however. He attacked Charles Kilgore Smith, the first secretary of Minnesota Territory, "without mercy." Smith was in Minnesota for only two years, and Goodhue went after him for that entire period with accusations of "fraud and malfeasance in office." Smith resigned in 1851 and moved back home to Ohio.

Goodhue also took aim at the bar. When the first court was held in the territory on August 12, 1849, he mocked the lawyers who had come in advance of a clientele. "The roll of attorneys is large for a new country. About 20, of the lankest and hungriest description, were in attendance."[45]

Despite his harshness in print, Goodhue faced no real opposition until a fateful winter day in 1851. On January 15, he wrote an editorial on the topic of "Absentee Office Holders."

While we regret the continued absence of a U.S. Marshal, and a judge of the 2nd district, from Minnesota, we would not be understood to lament the absence of A.M. Mitchell and David Cooper, the incumbents (oftener recumbents) of those two offices.—It would be a blessing if the absence of two such men were prolonged to eternity....We never knew an instance

*of a debt being paid by either of them, unless it were a gambling debt....
We never knew either of them, even to blunder into the truth, or to appear
disguised, except when accidentally sober...or to do anything right, unless
through ignorance how to do anything wrong.*

Judge Cooper, who was in consideration for chief justice of Minnesota, was "a miserable drunkard" who was "lost to all sense of decency and self respect. *Off* of the bench he is a beast, and *on* the bench he is an ass" (emphasis in original). Goodhue further accused him of sexually harassing a widow and of not mourning the death of his own wife. Goodhue castigated him and Mitchell for their paid advocacy in Washington, D.C., for the wheeler-dealer Henry M. Rice, a trader with the Ojibwes who was responsible for a tremendous acceleration of the St. Paul economy. Marshal Mitchell also received criticism from Goodhue for "cowardice." According to Goodhue, Mitchell's "least fault is drunkenness," and his "very name is a byword for contempt in Minnesota."

These were severe charges, but Goodhue insisted that he "uttered *truths* here, good wholesome truths; for the proof of which we stand responsible. It is our habit to tell facts and nothing else; and we have some *more* facts, 'a few more of the same sort left.'"[46]

After the paper had been distributed, Goodhue went about his daily work. He went to the brick building at the corner of Third Street and Washington that housed the territorial legislature and sat in on a session. When the proceedings finished, he left with a friend. They got only a few steps down the street when Judge Cooper's brother Joseph accosted them. Cooper took a swing at Goodhue. They both drew their guns, Goodhue a single-barrel pistol, Joseph Cooper a revolver. They argued, then Cooper announced, "'I'll blow your G[o]d d[amned] brains out." Sheriff Cornelius V.P. Lull ran over and took away their guns.

It wasn't over: Cooper had a knife, and Goodhue had another pistol, and they brandished their secondary weapons at each other. A well-meaning bystander tried to hold Goodhue back, and Cooper seized the opportunity to stab him in the abdomen. Goodhue jerked free of the man restraining him and shot Cooper, giving him a

Henry M. Rice. *Minnesota Historical Society: Minnesota Digital Newspaper Hub.*

"serious wound." Cooper rallied and stabbed Goodhue again, this time in his back. At last their friends were able to pull them away from each other and tend to their injuries. Both men survived. Witnesses agreed that Goodhue had acted in self-defense.[47]

Goodhue, writing in his paper about the incident, claimed that it was part of a conspiracy by his enemies to murder him and that Cooper had been egged on.

The denizens of St. Paul were horrified, and the town leaders held a community meeting, which gave the public some satisfaction. Goodhue did not back down in his journal, but he was not assaulted again. He also did not live much longer. He appeared to have made a full recovery but, in August of the following year, he died at the age of forty-two of a "terrible spasm" caused by latent damage from his stab wounds.[48]

THE MINNESOTA PIONEER

St. Paul, Minnesota,

Thursday Morning, January 16, 1851.

Absentee Office Holders.

While we regret the continued absence of a U. S. Marshal, and a judge of the 2d district, from Minnesota, we would not be understood to lament the absence of A. M. Mitchell and David Cooper, the incumbents (oftener recumbents) of those two offices.— It would be a blessing if the absence of two such men were prolonged to eternity. In the present scarcity and high price of whiskey, their absence may be considered a blessing. The loss by these men, of poor washer-women, laundresses, barbers, tailors, printers, shoemakers and all persons, with whom that sort of men make accounts, is quite as large already, as ought to fall to the share of the poor people in one Territory. We never knew an instance of a debt being paid by either of them, unless it were a gambling debt—and we never knew an act performed by either of them, which might not have been quite as well done by a fool or a knave. We never knew either of them, even to blunder into the truth, or to appear disguised, except when accidentally sober, or to do anything right, unless through ignorance how to do anything wrong, nor to seek companionship with gentlemen as long as they could receive the countenance of rowdies. Since the organization of the Ter-

This news story, "Absentee Office Holders," was the motive for James M. Goodhue's murder. *Library of Congress: Chronicling America.*

5
VIOLENCE AND TRAGEDY

The newcomers trickling, and then pouring, into St. Paul put a great strain on the once-small community. Even as the increased population brought money, skills and other resources, it also brought a class of rowdy adrenaline seekers, some of whom had come because they had burned their bridges back East, others because they were drawn by a romantic spirit of adventure. While St. Paul had not been innocent of violence before 1849, the town would see more tragedy in two years than it had experienced in the whole prior decade. The assault on Goodhue was but one incident of many.

The first trial for homicide in the Minnesota Territory came in September of that year. The defendant was a young man named Isaiah McMillan, who had killed another youth, Heman Snow, near the corner of Third and Franklin Streets. McMillan shot him right in the head.

The trial took place in Stillwater with District Court Judge David Cooper presiding. The jury found that McMillan had not acted with malice aforethought, and it "returned a verdict of manslaughter, with a recommendation to mercy."[49] Cooper sentenced him to one year in prison. There being no civilian jail at that time, he served his sentence in the Fort Snelling guardhouse but was given a certain degree of freedom by his guards. That sentence may seem like excessive leniency, but it was widely believed that McMillan had an intellectual impairment.

The next tragedy befell the young attorney David Lambert. Lambert, like Goodhue, had worked in the news business in Wisconsin, where he

Attorney David Lambert's ad ran in the paper for months after his death. *Library of Congress: Chronicling America.*

had been the editor and publisher of the *Madison Enquirer*. He had a talent for journalism but abandoned that career and moved to St. Paul in 1848, recognizing the promise of the riverside settlement. He was secretary of the Stillwater Convention, where he wrote the resulting memorial. He became a land agent while returning to the practice of law. His clientele included Henry M. Rice. St. Paulites were impressed with his gifts for both law and commerce. He had some personal difficulties, despite a "brilliant career," and turned for comfort to that substance for which St. Paul was infamous: whiskey. His "brain became disordered."[50] On November 2, 1849, Lambert threw himself off the roof of a steamboat and drowned. An advertisement he had put in the newspaper for Vetal Guerin's property continued to run through the spring of 1850, haunting readers with the memory of the town father who had destroyed himself around the age of thirty.

The horror would pick up in earnest in 1850. For such a small community, the number of violent incidents was high. In February, Alexander R. McLeod and William B. Gordon brawled on the Stillwater Road by Phelan's creek (later, Phalen Creek). Within twenty-four hours, Gordon died of his injuries. Justice John A. Wakefield set bail at the high price of $200. McLeod had an able legal defense in the person of Edmund Rice Jr., brother (and sometimes partner) of Henry M. Rice. Attorney Rice argued that his client had acted in self-defense. Both men had been drunk, and Gordon had struck first, using a steel wedge. McLeod had had nothing but his fists with which to defend himself and was lucky to escape with his life, given the weapon used against him. Gordon was acquitted.

Just two months later, Jacob R. Shipler "assault[ed] his wife with intent to kill,"[51] and he was sentenced to only one year's incarceration at Fort Snelling.

He escaped from the sheriff, then from the territory and subsequently from justice.

On July 4, the town of St. Paul saw its first lynching attempt. Judge Aaron Goodrich was doing his grocery shopping when he overheard a man amassing a mob to lynch the banker Charles W. Borup. Goodrich, a friend of Borup's, ran to the latter's home on the corner of Fourth and Jackson Streets to warn him. Borup barely had time to be alerted before the crowd was upon him. The ringleader "informed the banker that he had insulted…the whole American nation."[52] Borup was confused, but then he looked up at his flagpole and saw that the Union Jack waved instead of the flag of the

Alexander Ramsey. *Library of Congress Prints and Photographs Division.*

United States! Borup told the crowd that he had not known that the foreign flag was there. The crowd believed him and dispersed, but until he gave his explanation, they had been prepared to murder a man in broad daylight, the father of a six-year-old child. It was that child, incidentally, who had flown the flag without his father's knowledge after finding it in storage, a gift from a family friend who had lived in a British territory.

That same year, the territorial governor, Alexander Ramsey, learned of a conspiracy to burn him in effigy in front of his home. He would not take this insult lying down. He assembled his allies, gave them guns and took up his own weapons, a sword and a gun. He was prepared to do literal battle. He stationed his allies around the house and made sure that ammunition, additional armaments and food supplies for a siege were all in place. He and his friends were amped up for the confrontation to come. Ramsey paced his parlor, muttering quotes from *Macbeth*.

In the middle of the night, a sentinel posted outside called, "They come! They come!"[53]

Each man grabbed his gun, ready to fight to the death for the governor. It was a false alarm. No mob came. The men nodded off and woke near daybreak. They left Ramsey's house and proceeded to the Monk Hall saloon at the corner of Eagle and Exchange Streets. It was here that the effigy plot had allegedly been hatched. The governor's men smashed the windows with stones and chased out the occupants. Inside, they found the unused effigy.

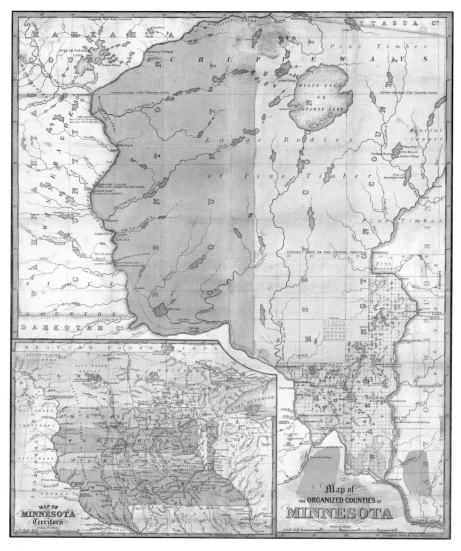

"Counties of Minnesota, 1850." *Hennepin County Library Digital Collections.*

ALTHOUGH THERE WERE AT this time many alcohol-related confrontations, only two ended in death in 1852. Chauncy Godfrey, from Wisconsin, shot his wife in the heart on July 21. She died quickly. They were living in the Tremont House, a small hotel on Bench Street. The neighbors overheard the gunshot as well as Godfrey's "fit of jealousy and drunkenness" that preceded it. He bolted before any of them could seize him. He was caught days later and incarcerated. He escaped after a few weeks and left the territory. "No effort to retake him was made, and he was never heard from again."[54]

The second murder was a disgrace to the settler community, if they had only realized it. In the Third Street saloon belonging to Thomas Caulder, a fight broke out on October 12. More than five men jumped into the fray. When the dust cleared, one of the men, Simon Dalton, lay dying of a stab wound. Among his assailants was an attorney, Daniel Breck, who had recently arrived from Kentucky. A coroner's jury could not determine who had wielded the knife, and all the men went free. "Maybe he suicided?" Williams mused sarcastically decades later.[55] Attorney Breck sauntered out of town, facing no consequences.

6
PULLED BY THE BLANKET

On May 15, 1850, twenty-five-year-old Hole in the Day hid his canoe at the mouth of the stream coming out of Wakan Tipi cave. He was no ordinary youth. He was an Ojibwe chief and the successor to his father, Hole in the Day (the Elder). It was close to noon. Hole in the Day and his companions waited in ambush for Dakotas from Kaposia, where Big Thunder's son His Scarlet Nation[56] was now chief. A few unfortunate men walked by, unawares, and Hole in the Day and his warriors rushed them. Hole in the Day killed and scalped a man, and the assailants retreated.

The settlers heard about it from frantic Dakotas, who were shouting back and forth across the river and running along the shore. They dropped their blankets and were nearly naked, but they were armed and angry. They ran off northward through St. Paul in pursuit of the Ojibwe attackers, but it was too late.[57] Hole in the Day and his friends arrived at their home eighty miles away and had a scalp dance.

This was revenge for a Dakota raid on an Ojibwe camp in Wisconsin a month earlier, for which Governor Ramsey, who also served as territorial superintendent of Indian Affairs, had had thirteen Dakota warriors arrested. They were currently being held at Fort Snelling. After Hole in the Day's raid, Ramsey decided not to pursue further action against those prisoners but instead to work it out between their leaders. He called for a council at Fort Snelling and opened with an abrasive speech in which he declared that the U.S. government was more powerful than they were, and he called for an end to the violence. (What he did not mention was that

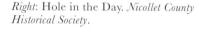

Left: His Scarlet Nation, also known as Little Crow. *Library of Congress Prints and Photographs Division.*

Right: Hole in the Day. *Nicollet County Historical Society.*

PO-GO-NAY-KE-SHICK, (HOLE IN THE DAY.)
The Celebrated Chippewa Chief.
WHITNEY'S GALLERY,   -   -   SAINT PAUL.

it was bad for business.) The chiefs present, including Hole in the Day, verbally agreed to the governor's demand that they stop fighting. Whether or not they intended to keep their word, the fact is that they fought again, many times.

The conditions of the Natives in Minnesota remained as difficult as before. To raise funds, they performed traditional dances in the streets of St. Paul, busking, and they stole from the settlers. Some of them resorted to eating garbage when they had nothing else. This is all the more distressing when one keeps in mind that, according to Larpenteur, they wasted nothing and were frugal with their resources.[58] It just wasn't enough.

On January 10, 1851, Hole in the Day addressed the Minnesota territorial legislature at the First Presbyterian Church. In an "eloquent and pathetic" speech, he "represent[ed] the starving condition of his tribe, and solicit[ed] relief for them."[59] The legislature appointed a committee to secure funds and accumulated donations. The small relief came too late. Many Ojibwes died of starvation that winter, and some who survived did so by cannibalism.

As for the Dakotas, Ramsey made it his mission to oppress them. When he had addressed the first legislative assembly back on September 3, 1849, five days short of his thirty-fourth birthday, he advocated building a military road to the Missouri River on which troops would march up and down once a year or more to intimidate the "wild Sioux" (that is, the Dakotas who had not adopted Euro-American culture).[60] Most importantly, "there was…one matter which Governor Ramsey knew to be of supreme interest to the whole people and that was the opening of the lands west of the Mississippi River"—Dakota land. Ramsey urged the territorial legislature to "memorialize [U.S.] Congress for the purchase of the whole Sioux country."[61] The legislators agreed, and they approved so heartily of the young governor's goals and efforts that they named the county after him during that session.

In fact, according to the historian and first president of the University of Minnesota, William W. Folwell, "from the May day of 1849 on which Ramsey arrived in Minnesota…there was not a day in which…he was not reminded that the one predominant and absorbing interest of the white people of the territory was the acquisition of the lands occupied by the Sioux Indians."[62] It was no coincidence that Ramsey had singled out "wild Sioux" to be the targets of military intimidation. His intention was to make it unpleasant for them to remain on their ancestral land.

Ramsey and Sibley had at first built their fortunes via competing avenues: Ramsey and his fellow real estate dealers needed the Natives gone in order to invest in their land; Sibley and his fellow traders needed them close by in order to profit from the annuity payments. They were political rivals—Ramsey was a Republican and Sibley was a Democrat—but they were sort of friends. Ramsey felt a strong platonic affection for Sibley that the latter did not reciprocate, and Sibley's allies would scheme about how they could use Ramsey's personal loyalty to their own advantage. In the case of the 1851 Dakota treaties, Ramsey did not need to be manipulated. He and Sibley had a common goal. They decided that the Dakotas had to be removed from as much land as possible while keeping them within the Minnesota Territory "so that their annuity money could support the territorial economy."[63]

Sibley was now a territorial delegate to Washington, D.C. He used his influence to get permission for himself, Ramsey and their associates to negotiate what they thought would be a final treaty.

The Dakotas themselves "had [had] in the year 1849 little desire for a treaty and less for any alienation of their lands."[64] But come 1851, they wavered, in need of the money and rations that a treaty would provide.

A number of chiefs accepted an invitation from the government to attend treaty councils. Those living farther north gathered at a council scheduled for late June at Traverse des Sioux, about seventy miles southwest of St. Paul on the Minnesota River. The negotiations were acrimonious, but at last the parties reached an agreement. One by one, the chiefs stepped up to sign the treaty. Each of them, as he walked away, was literally "pulled by the blanket" and pointed in the direction of another document for signature.[65] Joseph R. Brown gave them a pen, and they signed what came to be known as the "traders' paper," which, among other things, was an authorization for the United States to pay, from the annuity fund, a specified debt directly to the traders listed.[66] Nathaniel McLean, the Indian agent for the Dakotas, noticed this unexpected activity and asked to have the paper read and explained. This was refused. McLean, reviewing it later, thought that some of the sums supposedly owed to traders were fraudulent.

On August 5, there was a similar council in Mendota. A matter of contention for the Dakotas was something called the "education fund," a $15,000 perpetual annuity guaranteed in the terms of the 1837 treaty. "Education" sounds nice, but it had never been used in all that time, and yet it had been withheld from the Dakotas. Chief Wabasha raised the issue first, but it was His Scarlet Nation who, on the third day of negotiations, told Ramsey firmly, "We do not want to talk on the subject of a new treaty, until it is all paid." Ramsey interrupted with a pitiful counteroffer. His Scarlet Nation said only, "We will talk of nothing else but that money, if it is until next spring." In the following days, Wabasha and His Scarlet Nation drove a hard bargain on several points against Ramsey. At last, one of Ramsey's fellow commissioners, Colonel Luke Lea, remarked that they might "get hungry by too much talk."[67] It was a threatening reminder that the Dakotas had come to depend on annuities to sustain themselves. His Scarlet Nation and Wabasha had no choice but to sign the treaty, and once again Dakota leaders were tricked into signing a traders' paper.

The pot had been sweetened with an agreement by the commissioners that the whole $15,000 for the education fund would be paid in cash, with an extra $30,000 on top of it. "It was probably no accident," mused Folwell, that "the American Fur Company had that amount of specie on hand and at once advanced it to the Indian agent, who paid it out the next day." To the surprise of no one, "not many days passed before substantially the whole amount was in the hands of the traders and the merchants of St. Paul."[68] Almost immediately, and long before ratification, settlers flocked to the west bank of the Mississippi that was now ceded by the treaty. Ramsey "did nothing to stop the tide of immigrants and was happy to see small towns popping up across the land so recently taken from the Dakotas." Henry M. Rice, both in his store in St. Paul and at Traverse des Sioux, would persuade Dakota signatories to agree to later amendments to the treaty by misleading them about what the changes would entail. He allowed them to believe that the amendments would void the traders' paper. When they learned the truth from Ramsey in the autumn of 1852, they were furious, but their attempts to challenge the treaty process failed.

7

THE GOOD OLD DAYS

I n 1852, in a break from tradition, two St. Paulites were murdered by Dakotas. The first victim was Elijah Terry, a young man who was on his way to Pembina in modern-day North Dakota to work as a schoolteacher. His killers shot him first with a gun, then with arrows, and finally they scalped him. The second victim was Mrs. Keener. She and her friends were just north of Shakopee, which is about thirty miles southwest along the Minnesota River from St. Paul, when a group of Dakotas attacked them. One of the Dakotas, Yu-ha-zee, punched Mrs. Keener with his gun. A friend of hers then threatened him, and in defiance, Yu-ha-zee loaded his gun and fired on Mrs. Keener and wounded one of the others in her party.

Yu-ha-zee was held at Fort Snelling until the November term of the U.S. District Court. He was "escorted from Fort Snelling by a company of mounted dragoons in full dress." Yu-ha-zee was a sad sight in comparison, "half hid in his blanket, in a buggy with the civil officer, surrounded with all the pomp and circumstance of war." The jury returned a guilty verdict. When Judge H.Z. Hayner asked him if there were any reason why a death sentence should not be given to him, Yu-ha-zee answered through an interpreter that his village would exchange their annuities for his release. Hayner answered that he did not have the authority to permit that. After a stern statement, he "pronounced the first sentence of death ever pronounced by a judicial officer in Minnesota." Yu-ha-zee "trembled while the judge spoke, and was a piteous spectacle." [69]

That wasn't the only break in tradition, either. International violence came to town, after years of the various Native nations, Ho-Chunk, Ojibwe and Dakota, taking care to keep their raids on each other away from the heart of the settlement.

During the night of April 27, 1853, a group of Ojibwe men, sixteen or thereabouts, appeared in St. Paul. They were getting into position for a raid on the Dakotas. This was revenge. A war party from Kaposia had gone up to the St. Croix valley and killed a single Ojibwe, but two of His Scarlet Nation's sons died, too. That in turn was revenge for an Ojibwe attack near Shakopee on April 9, resulting in the death of a Dakota. The leader of the April 27 party was a young chief, A-luc-en-zis. He and his men hid in a vacant building in Lower Town. They rose with the sun and prowled the river bank, watching for Dakotas from Kaposia crossing the river. Finally, a canoe docked at the landing behind Jackson Street. It was Berry Picker, Rattler's sister. This morning, she was accompanied by one of her sisters and by one of their other brothers, Shelter Top, who was nicknamed "One-Legged Jim" thanks to an injury in a battle with Ojibwes.

A-luc-en-zis and his men followed one street behind them. As Berry Picker and her siblings were entering the Minnesota Outfit at the corner of Jackson and Third Streets, Auguste Larpenteur stood in front of the store diagonally across the corner, unpacking a shipment of crockery. He watched the Ojibwe warriors "crouching over, moving slowly, and holding their guns cocked but half-hidden beneath their blankets." Larpenteur dropped his plates as the men stopped across the street from the Outfit building and fired into the windows. Inside the Outfit, Shelter Top drew his pepperbox revolver, ran to the door and tried to fire back. The gun didn't go off. He threw it down. Larpenteur ran into the store, just in time to catch Berry Picker's sister as she fell, wounded. She had been shot in the back. "See, Wam-dus-ka," she said to Larpenteur, "I die."[70]

Berry Picker, also known as "Old Bets." *Minnesota Historical Society, Minnesota Digital Newspaper Hub.*

The Ojibwe warriors charged the store. Messrs. Borup and Oakes, who were also in the store, ran to confront them at the door, accusing the Ojibwes of cowardice for attacking women. Borup and Oakes managed to chase them off. By that time, Shelter Top had grabbed a loaded gun from the Outfit and ran after the Dakotas. He fired it, wounding A-luc-en-zis, though not severely. The chief fired back, knocking out a fragment from Shelter Top's wooden leg.

There was one other casualty, Antoine Findlay, who was grazed by a bullet but otherwise unharmed. Berry Picker's sister regained consciousness and asked to be brought home to Kaposia to die. She made it there and died within a few hours.

The shouting and gunshots had drawn a crowd of settlers, who, on being informed of what had happened, took off after the Ojibwes and caught up to them. "White man," said one of the warriors, "why do you pursue us? This is none of your affair! Do you mean to interfere in our fights?" The settlers were unarmed; the Ojibwes were armed. So the settlers had no choice but to let them go.

Ramsey ordered the Fort Snelling troops to go after them. Lieutenant W.B. McGruder led a cavalry platoon up to the St. Croix Falls, following the lead of a Dakota guide. According to the official account, the Ojibwes fired on the soldiers. The soldiers returned volley, and McGruder fired back, killing an Ojibwe man. A cavalryman scalped the corpse.

The next year, a reporter, the appropriately named Thomas M. Newson, came for a tour of Fort Snelling. He was in his mid-twenties, an orphan without any college education, but he had founded, owned and operated several newspapers back East. He had recently arrived in town, where he worked for Joseph R. Brown, who had taken over the *Pioneer* after Goodhue's death. Newson saw the scalp, still in the possession of McGruder. Newson was a very different man in temperament from the late Goodhue, having a more kindly disposition. Still, he cared as much for truth-telling as Goodhue had. Newson revealed a markedly different version of the abovementioned account: it was the soldiers who fired first, and they did so without orders.

There was much that his fellow St. Paulites preferred to sweep under the rug that Newson considered vital to keep in the public consciousness. For example, the December 1853 murders, one of which was yet another homicide in self-defense: Thomas Grieves, a "low desperado," attacked William Constans, a commission merchant on the levee, and Constans shot him to death.[71] But the following murders were far more gruesome and raised Newson's ire.

The day after Christmas, two young, "respectable and intelligent" mechanics, John Clark and Philip Hull, spent the early part of their evening in a saloon, where they chatted with each other for a while. They got up to leave, going out into the dark night, and one or more of the men who had also been in the saloon got up after them and went out as well. At the corner of Robert and Fifth Streets, a short walk from the saloon, Clark and Hull were attacked with a slingshot or something similar—or some*things* similar—and their skulls were broken. The killer or killers disappeared into the night. The victims took much longer to fade. Clark lingered in life until December 31; Hull expired on January 5. It appeared that, during their conversation in the saloon, the two victims had "unintentionally made some severe criticism on political or religious subjects, which must have given great offense to some persons in their hearing."[72]

In an editorial, "Foul Murder," printed on the day of Hull's death, Newson reminded his fellow St. Paulites:

This is the first case of premeditated murder that has occurred in our city, and the wanton barbarity of the act shows that we have among us some of the most depraved of our race....Two innocent, worthy young men have been murdered...cowardly, shamefully murdered!...We believe that there is sufficient moral power in this community...to strike terror in the hearts of [the killers]....*Our own security demands it; justice demands it; civilization demands it.*

He announced that A.M. Fridley, the new Ramsey County sheriff, had offered a $500 reward "for the apprehension of the party or parties guilty of the murder."[73]

At his office, Newson received two unexpected visitors, both clergymen. Newson recalled later: "They thanked [me] very sincerely for [my] courage, but expressed their fears that [I] might lose [my] life for thus daring...to speak out....They even desired to accompany me home."[74] Newson declined their offer. He was not assaulted.

Someone out there was so influential that a saloon full of witnesses was willing, by their silence, to protect them from the consequences of their violence. Writing in 1876, Williams said that it was widely known in the community who had committed the murder. He would not say who it was, as no one would give evidence against them. There was a citywide conspiracy among the town fathers to shield the killer or killers from justice.

Yu-ha-zee had received no such protection. Later that January, Newson attended his hanging on St. Anthony Hill, where a "hooting mob followed the poor creature to his death, on a cold and windy day." Yu-ha-zee had been "shabbily dressed" by his captors, and the spectators at the hanging made "vulgar and obscene remarks...when he was ushered into eternity."

Light Mixed Yellow,
T— ora, the White
White Flint, may be
st. Indeed all kinds
h a full perfect grain,
n properly tried.
not commenced grow-
yet, although it can
eat or Oats.
in has been grown con-
d is receiving the at-
ularly in the beautiful

ed only say that the
atoes are produced,
sota than any part of
asts of the size of her
y excel this Territory,
it exceedingly. It is
ble authority, that nu-
this year 400 bushels
they this fall that they
shel delivered in St.
Iinnesota must export
the southern, northern
Potatoe of Minnesota
ot, and cheaper in its
part of this confeder-
to any extent, made
or do we think it will.
, which warms quick-
ation faster than a clay
is adapted all things
nts of man. As an
dity with which vege-
climate, a gentleman
Radishes on the 1st
on his table on the 19th

grows in our soil to an
neasuring 13 inches in
was a large barrel of
9 inches in circumfer-
the acre I have not
it must be enormous,
aced in a few scattered

of this continent can
ed or a greater yield to
his vegetable, and its
, is produced in large
l other stock.
Radishes, Tomatoes,
bers, Water Mellons,
Pumpkins, Squashes,
e well in our soil and
ate and flavor, as any
e lower latitudes.
cannot have bearing
as it were, the land

Foul Murder.

On Monday night, the 26th ult. two of our citizens were assaulted near the corner of Roberts and
Fifth streets, by some person or persons who approached them from behind and felled them to the
earth with a slung-shot. Both the young men had
their sculls fractured in several places by the blows,
from the effect of which they have since died. Mr.
John Clark, one of the wounded men, expired on
Friday morning, the 30th, and Mr. Philip Hull, the
other, on Wednesday morning, the 5th.

This is the first case of premeditated murder that
has occurred in our city, and the wanton barbarity of
the act shows that we have among us some of the
most depraved of our race.

The young men were both respectable mechanics,
and both had money upon their persons, but it was
not molested. Neither of them could give any clue
by which the perpetrators of the deed could be traced.

These most malicious, unprovoked and diabolical
murders have aroused the public mind to a high state
of indignation bordering on frenzy, and imperatively
demand the energetic action of our officers and of every law-abiding, well-disposed citizen. Stringent measures should immediately be taken to ferret out the
perpetrators of the foul deed, for if such things are
permitted to go by without a thorough investigation,
other cases will transpire, and no citizen's life will be
secure against the hand of the midnight assassin.

"What of the night?" Two innocent, worthy
young men have been murdered—inhumanely mur-
dured—murdered in a civilized community—coward-
ly, shamefully murdered! Well may we inquire of
the watchman, "what of the night?" Well may
we pause and contemplate the effect of this savage
deed? Well may the heart sicken at the recital of
the sad tale. Well may we have sad forebodings for
the future, unless something is done to check the tide
of iniquity which is rolling in upon us. We believe
that there is sufficient moral power in this community, when once aroused, to strike terror in the hearts
of those who prowl about our streets in search of victims to rob and to murder, and if ever there was a
time to show that power, it is now—now, while the
blood of two of our fellow citizens cries for justice—
now, while the guilty consciences of the bloody vil-
lains are torturing their inmost souls—now, while
mourning friends are paying the last sad rites to the
departed dead. Our own security demands it; the
security of the community demands it; justice demands it; civilization demands it.

We are glad to learn that Sheriff Fridley has offered a reward of $500, " for the apprehension and
conviction of the party or parties guilty of the murder." It will also be seen by a notice in another
column, that a public meeting of the citizens to consider the matter, is called for Friday evening. Let
something be done to prevent, if possibly a repetition
of the horrible transaction we have been called upon
to record.

central between the I
Norway, and also bet
the Cape de Verde Isl
we have never observe
told it actually does ro
hours. No swamps a
ries, and where they o
variably surrounded I
abundant in the woods,
Territory produces all
pine saw-log to a ho
the winter break nor t
what time such things
in this Territory is gov
of the atmosphere for t
most in wet weather.
ter, and rises in the s
considered heavier tha
regular and uninterru
tween here and St. Lo
til the 20th of Novemb
mer there will probabl
steamers to and from
different railroad lines
the Pembina Dog Trai
passage from St. Louis
to fifteen dollars, acco
you have on hand, and
the boat. For the pr
west, we would respec
Delegation.

TERRITOFIAL A
Yesterday the Delegati
Agricultural Societies,
citizens, from various p
at the capitol, and orga
ral Society. The mer
ous than we anticipate
men practically acquain

It is a well understoo
Agricultural Societies
ting agricultural knowl
cultural interests of o
many European States,
and gratification we see
making for the promoti
and the development of

Much good has alre
the counties, by the fo
we hope to see every o
and efficient County So
ety contemplates a far l
the Territory what a lo
we expect the organiza
moting the agricultural
agricultural knowledge
We will give the p
of the Territorial Soci

ROADS.—We call th
communication in anoth

"Foul Murder," the news story that led two clergymen to fear for Thomas
Newson's safety. *Library of Congress: Chronicling America.*

Newson "denounced the proceedings." He did not doubt that Yu-ha-zee was guilty, but he was disgusted with the "alacrity and the manner in which he was punished, while many white murderers [had been] permitted to escape, without even any serious effort to arrest them."[75]

THE YEAR 1854 WOULD prove to be a tough one for journalists. Newson unintentionally courted danger in print again. He blasted Territorial Secretary J. Travis Rosser, a Virginian "lover of slavery and...hater of abolitionists," for "impos[ing] upon a colored man at the Capitol." Newson "stated that no gentleman would be guilty of the act imputed to [Rosser]," and this sent Rosser into such a frenzy that he announced that he would thrash Newson. Newson was worried enough about it that "of course I made preparation for my defense," but luckily Rosser let it go.

Once, after giving a speech on various topics including "corruption which ran knee-deep through our legislative halls," Newson was approached by six men, some of whom were important businessmen and politicians. They told Newson that they wished to accompany him home. Newson "learned that [his] life had been threatened by parties then in the room."[76] He considered this a sufficiently credible threat to allow them to escort him to his boardinghouse. Looking back on that era, Newson said, "I received many threats as to my being killed, horse-whipped, etc."[77] Nothing worse ended up happening to him than getting kicked for his involvement in bringing an end to a customhouse swindle.[78] "Twice I confronted men in my office with loaded revolvers, but for some cause or other the weapons didn't go off."[79] Newson was not alone in this. In 1854 and again in 1855, one of his colleagues was hunted on two separate occasions by an armed, angry man. The first one was a banker and the second was a politician.

Politicians could be rough-and-tumble, even the honest ones. Judge Goodrich and a member of the state legislature, Bill Davis, once held up another member at gunpoint outside the Capitol. The man had stolen a bill, proposed by Goodrich, to get rid of imprisonment for debt. In the past few years, one debtor had died in prison and another had essentially gone into exile because he could not pay his creditors. The thief pretended at first not to know what they meant. "You have the bill now in your pocket," said Goodrich. "If this be not so, hold me responsible." Davis resorted to threats and cursing. When that didn't work, he drew and cocked his pistol, took out his watch and said that he would shoot in two minutes. The thief handed over the bill. Newson believed that if he had not done as they told him, "he would have been a dead man, for in those days men meant what they said when they drew a pistol on another."[80]

These were wild times, but before too long, St. Paulites would look back on them with nostalgia.

8
CARNIVAL OF CRIME

S t. Paul had a banner year in 1855. A wave of business activity that had taken off in 1854 continued to rise, as did immigration, thanks to a combination of steamboat navigation and rail transportation, as the Chicago and Rock Island Railroad now reached the Mississippi River. There were 4,716 St. Paulites. The price of land increased, and "a speculative era rapidly set in." J. Fletcher Williams and the Reverend Edward D. Neill exaggerated when they wrote that "everybody possessed land and all equally had visions of great wealth," but they was correct in spirit: enough people fell into this category to alter the territory's economy: "An eminently unhealthy and artificial state of affairs was growing: the rate of interest was extremely high....More buildings were put up....Speculators...among all classes of the community...were selling lots at almost fabulous advances on the original purchase price."[81] It was a heady time in this town, with no apparent downside. There was natural beauty, easy money and a growing community. In that entire year, there was not a single murder.

By the end of 1856, the residential population had nearly doubled, and close to twenty-eight thousand people had registered at hotels.[82] Not all of the latter group were transients. Some of them were waiting for their homes to be built so that they could move in. Business kept on booming, and so did a "carnival of crime."[83]

On June 26, the druggist William W. Hickcox, who owned a drugstore and an illicit saloon at Third and Cedar Streets, got into an altercation with a drayman named Peltier. He had told Peltier to bring up some items from the Robert Street wharf to the store. Peltier got to the store with the goods later than Hickcox had expected, and they argued about the timing and the cost of the haulage. As far as the police could tell, "No one will ever [know who] struck the first blow" in the fight that followed.[84] Peltier finally lifted a dray pin and dealt Hickcox a fatal blow over the head. Peltier fled to his home, where the police broke in and arrested him. He was acquitted on the grounds of self-defense.

Aside from that affray, "the rush of immigration, and the fast habits induced by the speculative era, brought to our city numbers of thieves, gamblers and other abandoned characters."[85] As crime so often does, it worsened in summertime. On July 9, George R. McKenzie, owner of the Mansion House hotel, was found dead in the river, his pockets emptied of the cash he had been carrying when he left. Around the same time, Robert Johnson suffered a hideous death at the hands of highway robbers: they threw him, still alive, over the bluff. He did not survive the fall.

Johnson's murder was a watershed. At the public meeting that followed, the community appointed a vigilante group to patrol the streets at night. The city police had only four men, while the "secret police," as Williams called them, had many more. The vigilantes were efficient: "A number of suspicious characters [were] arrested and sent out of town, others tried for offenses committed, and punished, and security and order established in a short time."[86]

Incidentally, security and order also lasted only a short time. On January 14, 1857, the body of Henry William Schroeder was found in his tailor shop on West Third Street. Newson could picture it vividly nearly three decades later: "I see him still! [S]o pale, so horrible! He sits on his work table; the hand with the needle has stopped on its way to the garment which lies in his lap; his eyes glare; his face is so white—he's dead! [K]illed by an axe or a hatchet in the hands of an assassin."

Schroeder was unmarried and had not lived long enough in St. Paul to have made friends. He had "met his horrible fate a stranger in a land among strangers."[87] It was known that Schroeder kept his money with him, not in the bank, and so the motive was probably robbery. Said Williams, "No clue to the perpetrator of the atrocious act was ever discovered."[88]

Violence erupted in May, as steamboats full of rowdy tourists and rough roustabouts came in greater numbers with the warming weather. Brawls and highway robbery became daily occurrences. Drowning followed drowning, most likely involving alcohol. A young policeman, Andrews, was brutally assaulted during a riot early that month. He nearly died from his injuries.

ANOTHER VICTIM.—We are informed that Andrews, the policeman beaten by a mob on Minnesota street on the night of the election, is dangerously hurt, and is not expected to recover.

THE RAIN, AND OTHER SUBJECTS.—Yesterday was a *blue* day, and no news stirring. A dull drizzly rain was falling most of the time, which put a damp-er on everything out of doors, and rendered traveling almost out of the question. The item market was flat, and our note book was almost untouched by the pencil. It was too cold to sit in an office without fire, too disagreeable to be on the street, and too muddy at the wharf to tempt a news hunter to that locality. A perfect blankness reigned, or rather *rained*, over everything.—Complaints loud, and deep, and bitter were heard muttered against the weather, poor thing, and against everything else. It soured every body. Alas that mankind is so fickle! Wednesday it swore roundly at the dust which filled everybody's eyes, and choked everybody's lungs; and yesterday anathemas were hurled at the mud as everybody splashed along in *it*. Equanimity was out of the question. Every one's face wore a cloudy expression, like unto the dull leaden sky above. A mail which came in was the only relief we experienced. For a time, the mud, weather and all the ills were forgotten, until a malignant steam whistle sounded, and a trip to the wharf undertaken in pure desperation relieved us for a season. Really, a few such days in succession would seriously injure the lead pencil business, of which a local is an excellent supporter.

is entirely ready to start, with the exception of the purchase of the outfit, for which purpose Col. Nobles has not yet received the appropriation. The official members of the party are Capt. Devere, Sam. A. Medary, Engineer, and Mr. Fish; in addition to whom a strong force of assistants will be employed. The Expedition will proceed from Fort Ridgley, the starting point of the Route, as soon this spring as vegetation is far enough advanced to support the stock they will have with them.

A MAN DROWNED.—On Saturday morning, as a deck hand on board the steamboat Henry Clay was adjusting a line from the boat on shore, the line warped, and knocked him in the water. He passed under the boat and was drowned. His name was Mat. Cunningham.

THE local of the Pioneer says the trees on the opposite side of the river are beginning to *leave*! We should like to know their destination, neighbor Ramaly? Wonder that the owners don't attempt to detain them.

FATAL ACCIDENT.—Yesterday morning as two men were engaged in taking down the building formerly used as a drying kiln opposite the Jackson st. Methodist church, it fell in, and fatally wounded one of them. His skull was fractured badly, and some internal wounds were received, which makes it almost certain that he cannot recover. The other escaped without any injury. We could not learn his name.

A SARTORIAL ITEM.—The Journeymen Tailors of this city have been on a strike for several days, for an increase of wages, and we un-

A sample of news items in the local column of a St. Paul paper in May 1857, from the same issue in which the account of Peter W. Trotter's murder appeared. *Library of Congress: Chronicling America.*

Another policeman was injured while trying to break up an interethnic brawl, Irish versus German. The vast majority of these incidents did not end in deaths. There were successful shootings and stabbings, but wounds were patched and bullets removed.

Not so for Peter W. Trotter. On Saturday, May 9, 1857, Mike Smith, second mate of the steamboat *Progress*, was ready for a night on the town. With his friends, the first mate and some crewmembers, he got into a yawl, a small boat, and left the *Progress*, which was docked at the levee. They

took the boat upriver to the Cave, a notorious brothel just outside of town. There they met Trotter, who had come with some fellow lodgers from the Minnesota House hotel, which stood at Fifth and Wabasha. The men spent the evening drinking and dancing with the prostitutes. Around 10:00 p.m., the male bartender and one of the prostitutes observed Smith and Trotter in a "trivial altercation." Trotter remarked to the woman, "The d[amne]d son of a b[itch] [has] a pistol."[89] Smith grabbed him, and they fought in earnest. Smith drew a bowie knife with a nine-inch-long, double-edged blade. He stabbed Trotter in the leg and thigh. Trotter staggered off wordlessly, leaving a trail of blood behind him. He made it about 150 feet before dropping dead. His femoral artery had been severed.

The rivermen fled to their yawl. Trotter's friends ran down to St. Paul. They found a policeman, Officer Morton, and persuaded him to come to the levee to arrest the killer when he returned to the *Progress*. A few citizens and a town watchman went as well and waited at the upriver edge of the levee. After a few minutes, a yawl crawled up alongside the *Progress*, and a small group of men got out. A second yawl approached, holding only two men, one of whom was the killer. A few of the men on the shore told Morton that they would help him to arrest them. He not only turned down their help but also refused to make an arrest. The two men rowed away. It took some browbeating on the part of the impatient onlookers, but Morton finally, with their help, arrested the boatmen who had returned to the wharf and brought them to jail. Judge Orlando Simons examined them and determined that there was no evidence against them. They had been in the wrong place at the wrong time.

Peter Trotter was "well dressed, and respectable looking, and apparently 24 or 25 years old." He had been in town only one week. He had come from Iowa, where he worked as a butcher. Those last two facts were known only because of papers found in his possession after his death. He had had no friends in St. Paul. The coroner saw to his burial.

Officer Morton was excoriated in the press for letting Smith escape. Said the *Weekly Minnesotian*, "Mr. Morton…was repeatedly solicited and urged to pursue them.…Had the officer done what no one will deny was his duty, the real murderer might now be lodged in our jail." But the significance of this "Gross Neglect of Duty," as the headline called it, ran deeper: "No wonder that riot, and bloodshed, and violence, and *murder* even stalk before our eyes unrestrained, when men sworn to suppress them neglect, and even refuse to do their duty" (emphasis in original). The editorial concluded: "Our police organization ought to be overhauled, and such direlict [*sic*] officers expelled from the department, or impeached before the proper authorities for neglect of duty. If this were done, and good and true men put in their places, riots, mobs and murders would be less frequent or almost unheard of."[90]

The reporter was expressing a general sentiment, but some citizens, including his colleague Newson, were not willing to wait for administrative changes. Newson attended a community meeting that became an arson mob. They stormed the Cave, removed the furniture and valuables, "drove out" the prostitutes who lived and worked there and then set the building on fire. Newson watched as the home of innocent women went up in flames. When it had burned itself out, he and his fellow arsonists "deliberately walked home."[91]

Mike Smith was never caught.

In August, two city blocks were torched in separate acts of arson, one of them on Third Street, another on Robert Street near Fourth. These were *not* brothels, and the community strongly disapproved. There was a rash of burglaries, too. Another vigilance committee was organized. It was "thorough in its work" (likely a euphemism for "brutal"), but it was effective, and it made St. Paul less convenient for crime.

9

THE TERRIBLY HARD TIMES

T hroughout that summer, 1857, "St. Paul was said by travelers to be the fastest and liveliest town on the Mississippi River." So many people came to town by riverboat that the "stores were overtaxed…[and] hotels and boarding houses were crowded to overflowing."[92] Construction laborers worked around the clock, so great was the demand for new buildings for homes and retail and for street-grading and pipe-laying. The saloons and livery stables "coined money.…The city was continually full of tourists, speculators, sporting men, and even worse characters, all spending gold as though it was dross."[93]

From 1855 onward, the real estate market in St. Paul had grown at an exponential rate. With the shrinkage of the Fort Snelling reservation as the perceived need for a military defense in the immediate area faded, there was more real estate to go around in the vicinity of St. Paul. The city acreage increased, along with the price of land. Beyond this, there were copious deals made for land in farther-flung parts of the territory.

Newson remembered it as the force of water, apt for a resident of a river city: "The speculative real estate wave which started in 1855 and swelled to huge proportions in 1856 broke out into tremendous white-caps in 1857."[94] The real estate crash had to come at some time, as anyone with any distance from it could have guessed. "Almost every body went into the business of buying and selling real estate…[at] fabulous prices. It became a mania."[95] A good deal of false advertising went into it:

On paper these [Minnesota] cities (there were no towns,) looked elegantly well with their court house squares, and parks, and churches, and school houses, and steamboats, and railroad trains, and though the lots were located in marshes and in many cases in water, yet that, unknown to the purchasers, did not prevent the ignorant from buying, and so the wave rolled on, gaining force and carrying with it good, honest men, as well as bad men and robbers.[96]

Some of the sellers were predatory, some of the buyers were foolhardy. Governor Willis A. Gorman, Alexander Ramsey's successor, made an offer on some land for $10,000, a price far above its value. The assumption was that the value could only increase. It did not.

"No description," said J. Fletcher Williams, "that can be given of this singular era of our history can convey an idea of it, i.e., the buying of real estate…almost absorbed every other passion and pursuit."[97] A class of con men arose, "flourish[ing] in Saint Paul by the score," many of whom didn't even bother with an office. They didn't have any capital to start with, aside from a roll of maps and blank land deeds. They made so bold as to board boats coming into the levee or

hang around hotels, and, by a little sharp maneuvering…find out and manipulate unsuspecting strangers, who had money, and fleece them of their means, by selling them lots in moonshine towns, for several hundred dollars each, not actually worth as many cents, even if they got a title at all.[98]

"The whole tendency of this speculative land era was bad," said Newson.[99] Williams went further: "This mad, crazy, reckless spirit of speculation…was appalling, to look on it now from a soberer stand-point."[100] Williams mused, "Perhaps in no city of America, was the real estate mania, and reckless trading and speculation, so wild and extravagant, as in Saint Paul." It was not sustainable, "and must soon bring its own punishment in general ruin. Indeed, the storm was near at hand."[101]

The storm didn't come from St. Paul. It came from New York, where, on August 24, 1857, the Ohio Life Insurance and Trust Company failed, creating a domino effect that struck down economies across the country and internationally. This was known as the Panic of 1857, and it was the fastest-spreading financial crisis the United States had ever seen. Its impact on St. Paul was not immediately felt. The city had more pressing things on its mind, like yet another murder trial, after a man was beaten to death, and an assault by Governor Gorman on Thomas Wilson, a lawyer from Winona, that could have resulted in murder, as Gorman had smashed his ebony cane over Wilson's head. Wilson's offense? Answering, "most certainly," when Gorman asked him if he had little confidence in his (Gorman's) judgment.[102]

The *Weekly Minnesotian* broke the news from New York on September 12, printing a story from the *New York Herald*: "The Financial Crisis—No Cause for Alarm," the headline assured readers. According to the *Herald*, the "crisis" would affect no one aside from the Ohio Company and stock traders.[103] This prediction could not have been more wrong. The crash affected communities all over the country. The 1850s had been a prosperous decade until then, and corporations of all sizes, and people of all income levels had been investing their money, always expecting to make more. State and city governments issued railroad bonds, all for the sake of railways that never materialized. In Minnesota, Sibley had warned against that very thing, but Ramsey and his cronies endorsed the railroad companies to an extent that would make his contemporaries and historians look at him askance.

Williams recalled, "To Saint Paul, [the] pricking of the bubble of speculation was more ruinous and dire in its consequences than perhaps to any other city in the west. Everything had been so inflated and unreal... that the blow fell with ruinous force." The community was devastated, as "business was paralyzed, real estate actually valueless...and but little good money in circulation....The notes secured by mortgages must be paid, but all values were destroyed" and "all classes [were] in debt." Banks closed. Stores closed. The building industry ground to a halt. A "general gloom and despondency settled down on the community. In a few days, from the top wave of prosperity, it was plunged into the slough of despond."[104]

And then, said Newson, "came the terrible hard times! With no money, no values, no property, no business, little or no emigration [*sic*: he likely meant "immigration"], no banks, or banks with empty vaults." There was nothing to attract newcomers to the city, and it wrecked St. Paulites. "[There was] no courage, no hope, notes due, mortgages foreclosed, men heavily in debt, land depreciated from fifty to seventy-five per cent., no trade." Minnesotans in general had been so preoccupied with *selling* the land that they had not been *working* the land. They had been importing their produce, had nothing of their own to sell and were not even close to self-sufficient. "No one can imagine the frightful condition of affairs in ST. PAUL in the latter part of the year 1857 but he who passed through it all." Newson estimated that 90 percent of the settlers who lost their shirts in the crash never recovered, or if they did, it was not for a long time to come.[105]

The newspapers were full of foreclosure notices. Newson believed that fewer than 20 percent of businesses survived, no matter how hard their operators tried, and that St. Paul had lost 50 percent of its population. In May of the following year, 1858, Minnesota became a state. It was mired in debt. The federal government had authorized a $250,000 loan over the winter, but it was a long time coming. The state and its people were broke. Some of them used treasury warrants, but those bore interest. At the local level, cities and towns had their own scrip (a provisional money certificate). There was no genuine money to be found. There was still talk of the as-yet speculative railroads that had so far lined pockets but not laid tracks, and some banks opened on the basis of railroad bonds. Their issues reached the whole state but "were regarded with considerable distrust from the outset. Bankers in the state received this with much disrelish, and generally at a discount."[106] They had been right to be wary. In early June, "the brokers of the state…combined to depreciate the [railroad currency]." Soon, it was worthless. The railroad companies had formally ceased construction work, after the state had already issued $2,257,000 in bonds. In October, bonds were being sold at $0.10 on the dollar. As for the local scrips, they depreciated to as low as $0.50 on the dollar by winter of that year.

St. Paul dragged itself up. It was as well positioned geographically as it had always been, and now that landowners in the city and in the rest of the state were more interested in making do with what they had than in selling it, they began to cultivate their crops. The St. Paulites who stayed were the ones committed to their community. They could have gone to seek their fortunes elsewhere or returned to kin back East. St. Paul would survive. Not all of the recession's victims would, however.

On November 10, 1860, William C. Gray, who had been "a prominent broker and real estate dealer" and now served on the board of education, was arrested for forgery. He had tried to make up the differences in his losses through criminal means. Gray broke free of the sheriff, ran to the Wabasha Street Bridge and threw himself into the river. He wasn't the only St. Paulite to commit suicide in the wake of the '57 crash.

Henry McKenty had come to St. Paul from Pennsylvania in 1851 at the age of thirty. He was already an experienced, successful real estate dealer, bringing his own capital into the city. Newson recalled admiringly that McKenty "led off [St. Paul] in his special department as the great warrior of his profession. He was pre-eminently king!" Williams agreed. "McKENTY [was] the king of real estate dealers…on the flood-tide of prosperity."[107] Newson approached McKenty in 1853, even before the

View of the south side of downtown St. Paul from the Wabasha Street Bridge, from which William C. Gray leapt to his death. (The bridge, now officially—but not commonly—known as Wabasha Street Freedom Bridge, has been rebuilt twice since then). *Author's collection.*

"mania" had taken off. Newson had no cash, but he had an expensive watch to trade. He bought from McKenty a lot worth 20 percent of the value of his watch. Such was the faith that St. Paulites had in land values at that innocent time. Newson later "lost sight" of the lot, perhaps assuming after the crash that the deed wasn't worth the paper it was written on, only to discover more than twenty years later that it might be valuable.[108]

McKenty had a personality to match his ambitions. In the same year that he had accepted young Newson's watch, he also "secured" land in present-day Minneapolis. He heard that there were men who planned to overbid him at the land sale. He ordered two black coffins from a cabinetmaker and hired an omnibus and a band. He arrived at the sale, music playing, flags waving, with a bus full of people. He set the coffins on the ground, set two pistols on them and then stood on top of one of the coffins. "Now go on with your bidding!" he shouted. Nobody dared bid against him.[109]

By 1853, McKenty was making returns of 58 percent on land investments. In 1854, he "entered" thousands of acres of land in Washington County by land warrant (a certificate authorizing an individual person to take

"Fishing Boats at Lake Como." *Hennepin County Library Digital Collections.*

possession of a specified piece of public land) for $1.25 per acre; he sold them the next year for $5.00 per acre. He made $23,000.00 from that venture.[110] He reinvested it in more land, making money hand over fist. At one point he owned almost all of the land around Lake Como. To increase the accessibility, and therefore the value, of that real estate, he spent $6,000.00 on a public road.

McKenty did not really begin to feel the pinch until a year or so after the 1857 crash, or else he kept his suffering to himself as he sank into debt. One day, Newson was walking down Third Street and saw that the windows in McKenty's office door were shattered. Newson went in and asked the land dealer what had happened. "Oh, nothing, nothing much, sir; only a big dog, sir, went through that window, sir! Bad dog, sir! bad dog, sir!" McKenty smiled "serenely." Newson the nosy newsman went a few doors down and learned that a "pugnacious" character, Mr. Baker, had been hounding McKenty about a debt the latter owed him, and so McKenty picked him up by the seat of the trousers and hurled him through the window.[111]

McKenty kept up his office at Third and Cedar, and he also kept up his smile. Only close friends could tell that he seemed sad. Newson found an opportunity to give him money by making an absurdly high offer for a broken rocking chair. McKenty recognized it as charity and reverse-haggled, refusing to accept too much cash for it. He came to Newson's home one evening and sold him on some oil land. Newson coughed up $400 and received nothing back on his investment. McKenty had lost his touch.

On August 9, 1869, Newson and a friend of his saw McKenty at the Merchants Hotel, reading a newspaper upside down. They invited him to dinner, where he spent his time catching flies instead of talking. The next day, he shot himself to death. One of his daughters died soon after that, and then Mrs. McKenty hanged herself, leaving their remaining daughter alone in the world. She left St. Paul, the city that had taken so much from her family.

PART III

LOW LIGHTS, SMALL CITY

10
INAUGURAL HANGING

Stanislaus Bilansky was an immigrant pioneer. Originally from Poland, he claimed a plot of land between Phalen Creek and Trout's Brook in 1842 at the age of thirty-five. By September 1858, having lived continuously in St. Paul, he had not made a single close friend, despite being acquainted with all, as he was a saloonkeeper and grocer. He did, however, have two ex-wives and had just remarried. His new wife, Mary Ann Evans Bilanksy, was a striking, vivacious woman in early middle age who had recently moved to St. Paul from North Carolina. With a firm mind of her own, she had no fear of her husband, who might be compared in temperament to his fellow early settler Phelan. Unlike Mr. Bilansky's prior wives, the force of Ann's personality was such that he did not dare mistreat her. However, she was not a bully, and she got along with her four stepchildren, of whom she was effectively sole caregiver.

Why she married Bilansky is a mystery. Not only was he unpleasant and unhandsome, he was also living in poverty. Like many St. Paulites (the ones who had not had their mortgages foreclosed), he owned property but was cash poor, and he had had to close the grocery store and bar. His health was also poor, owing in large part to his alcoholism. His house, into which both the saloon and grocery store had been built, was infested with rats from a nearby flour mill. There were of course the children to tend to as well, and so Mrs. Bilansky was tasked with childcare on top of housekeeping, while her husband was either sickly or off on hunting trips.

All was not well. Mrs. Bilansky's relationship with John Walker was a constant point of contention between her and her husband. Walker, an attractive young carpenter, was also from North Carolina. He was the reason that Mrs. Bilansky had come to St. Paul in the first place. He got sick early in 1858, becoming almost bedridden, and had written to her to ask her to come nurse him. She soon had him well again, and he introduced her to his neighbors as his aunt. One of those neighbors was Stanislaus Bilansky. He and Ann were married in a matter of months.

Against Mr. Bilansky's wishes, but because Mrs. Bilansky willed it, Walker lived in a shack in the back of their property. Also against the husband's wishes, Walker and Mrs. Bilansky took a trip to the city of St. Anthony (which later became the East Bank of Minneapolis). In November, two months after the Bilanskys' wedding, one of Mr. Bilansky's children told him that he had seen his stepmother visiting Walker at night while Mr. Bilansky was away on a hunting trip. The boy may have been too young to understand the implications.

Stanislaus went hunting again, in December, and became ill. It took him a short while to recover. His health did not last long, and in February 1859, he declined so sharply that, in spite of their poverty, Ann hired household help so that she could devote more time to caring for him without worrying about other tasks.

Rosa Scharf, a young housekeeper, started her employment at the Bilansky home on March 2. Mr. Bilansky, she observed, was feverish, vomiting and forever thirsty. He deteriorated quickly. Mrs. Bilansky had initially been hesitant to call in a doctor, but on March 6, Dr. Alfred Berthier examined her husband. Mr. Bilansky himself was not worried. He believed that his symptoms were caused by getting his feet wet in the woods during his most recent hunting trip and from eating a heavy diet. Dr. Berthier instructed him to drink absinthe and water before meals and to eat a lighter diet.

Mr. Bilansky also had remedies of his own. He had a preexisting inclination toward quack medicines that he consumed out of a combination of hypochondriacal anxiety and as an effort to manage the long-term effects of heavy drinking. He turned to one of these medicines, Graffenburg pills.

Mrs. Bilansky, in compliance with the doctor's orders, provided a change in diet, of easily digested foods like soup and toast. But no matter what he ate, Mr. Bilansky could not tolerate it. His stomach always felt like it was burning, and it got worse when he ate. He'd throw it back up again. John Walker brought him some arrowroot to see if it would help, but it didn't.

Through it all, Mrs. Bilansky stayed by his side. Rosa Scharf observed that the husband and wife got along well. Mrs. Bilansky fussed constantly over her husband and would allow no one else to care for him, doing everything herself. And he needed a lot of care. He was capable of walking around in the home but was mostly in bed. He died on March 11 after drinking some liquor his eldest son had brought to him at his request.

Mrs. Bilansky couldn't afford the costs of the burial, and so Walker covered the expenses. As they were about to go to the cemetery on the afternoon of Saturday, March 12, Ramsey County officials, with the coroner, Dr. John V. Wren at the helm, interrupted the funeral procession. The body was examined, and the house was searched. The authorities interviewed John Walker and Miss Scharf, as well as Mrs. Lucinda Kilpatrick, who lived across the street from the Bilanskys. The coroner's jury heard their testimony. The jurors concluded that it was a death by natural causes and criticized Mrs. Bilansky for not calling the doctor back during the last few days. This was all wrapped up within a few hours, and Stanislaus Bilansky's mourners, such as they were, buried him at 5:00 p.m.

Later that day, Mrs. Kilpatrick told her husband that she and Mrs. Bilansky had gone shopping two weeks before Mr. Bilansky's death. At the drugstore, Mrs. Bilansky bought some arsenic. She told Mrs. Kilpatrick that they had given away their cat, and rats were invading the cellar in its absence, so Mr. Bilansky wanted her to buy arsenic to poison them. Mrs. Kilpatrick also said that the reason she had refrained from testifying to this at the inquest was that Mrs. Bilansky was hiding in the room, concealed behind a curtain, for the express purpose of listening in on Mrs. Kilpatrick's testimony. The next morning, Mr. Kilpatrick went to John Crosby, the St. Paul chief of police, to relay to him what he had heard from his wife.

Mr. Bilansky's body was exhumed that same day, Sunday, March 13, and John Walker and Ann Bilansky were arrested on suspicion of murder. Dr. Thomas R. Potts, a local politician and brother of Henry H. Sibley's second wife, performed the autopsy. He found no apparent evidence of poisoning but also no confirmation that Bilansky had died of natural causes. Dr. Wren ordered chemical analyses and, on March 18, called back to his City Hall office the same jury from Saturday.

Mrs. Kilpatrick testified again, this time telling them about the trip to the drugstore. She further testified, "I do not know anything about the man named Walker," only that she had seen him on Friday and did not know if he was or was not a relative of Mrs. Bilansky. But she knew some things about the Bilansky marriage and said that "Mrs. B[ilansky] told me she lived very unhappy with Mr. B[ilansky]. She said she hated him, and could not treat him well."[112]

Rosa Scharf testified that she had seen no rats in the Bilansky home, nor had she seen anyone set out poison for them, and that Mrs. Bilansky had not seemed sad that her husband was dead and that she had speculated that if he had been poisoned, suicide was the cause.

The physicians who performed the postmortem examination testified that there was inflammation in parts of Stanislaus Bilansky's lower digestive tract. The postmortem included the heart, kidneys and lungs, finding them to be healthy. They saw no positive evidence that he had died of alcohol poisoning. A druggist, William H. Wolff, along with Dr. William H. Morton, had conducted an experiment using the stomach contents. Wolff explained that they did not have the capabilities in St. Paul for a definite test for arsenic, but they did find *indications* of the presence of arsenic.

The jury concluded "that the deceased came to his death from poison administered to him by his wife, Ann Bilansky, between February 28, and March 10, 1859."[113] Walker was released. Mrs. Bilansky was charged with first-degree murder and then indicted on May 21. The trial commenced two days later. She was represented by a celebrity lawyer, the Yale-educated former Minnesota territorial legislator and former mayor of St. Paul John B. Brisbin and his colleague, A.L. Williams, former partner of Daniel Breck, who had been involved in the murder of Simon Dalton in the October '52 bar brawl.

In his sensational opening statement, Isaac V.D. Heard, the earnest young Ramsey County Attorney, started with the purchase of arsenic, the means by which, he said, Mrs. Bilansky committed the murder. He then said that Mrs. Bilansky was not Walker's aunt but instead his lover and that their affair was the motive for killing Mr. Bilansky. Finally, said Heard, Mrs. Bilansky had said things that suggested she was planning murder.

Mr. Heard first called Lucinda Kilpatrick to the stand. Her testimony matched what she had told the coroner's jury. Counselor Brisbin asked her, in the cross-examination, if she had had lots of sex partners. Heard objected to this, and Judge Edward C. Palmer sustained. Brisbin did manage to get some suggestive testimony regardless: Mrs. Kilpatrick admitted that she and Walker had been friends and that the friendship had come to an end more than a month earlier. Brisbin entered into evidence some affectionate but anonymous letters, as well as a ring and a breastpin that had been in Walker's possession. He asked Mrs. Kilpatrick if she had been the one to give them to Walker. She did not deny it, but she would not answer any further questions. Overruling an objection from Brisbin, Judge Palmer said that Mrs. Kilpatrick did not have to respond to this line of questioning.

Miss Scharf testified that Mrs. Bilansky had some peculiar household rules. First, Miss Scharf was not to use utensils that Mr. Bilansky had touched; second, Mrs. Bilansky washed all of her husband's dishes by herself and stored them separately from the rest of the dishware. This was perplexing to Miss Scharf, who was, after all, domestic help. Why was Mrs. Bilansky insistent on performing this task herself?

Miss Scharf also related a strange anecdote. One time, she and Mrs. Bilansky saw an old man walking past, and Mrs. Bilansky told Miss Scharf that she should marry him because he was rich. Miss Scharf replied that she wasn't interested, and Mrs. Bilansky told her that if she didn't love him, she could poison him. She suggested several options, arsenic among them. Perhaps most disturbingly, Miss Scharf testified that, when it appeared to her that Mr. Bilansky was dying, she offered to run over to the Kilpatricks' home across the street and ask them for help, but Mrs. Bilansky told her that there was no need to hurry.

Miss Scharf then testified that on the morning after Mr. Bilansky's death, Walker came to visit and "they did not look natural" (i.e., they behaved in an "unnatural," or inappropriate, manner).[114] She also gave her opinion that Mrs. Bilansky did not treat Mr. Bilansky "as I think a husband should be treated."[115] Then, on the night after the funeral, Miss Scharf witnessed Mrs. Bilansky undressing in front of Walker. According to Miss Scharf, Mrs. Bilansky donned nightclothes in the bedroom while Walker prepared for bed in the barroom. The adjoining door was open. However, as Miss Scharf and the Bilansky children were present, one may infer that this was a distinctly unsexy occasion. Walker would sleep on the barroom floor, while the women and children slept in the bedroom. Even at the time, though, Miss Scharf was uncomfortable enough to comment on it, and instead of changing into nightclothes, she merely stripped off her dress and slept in her underwear, which she considered a more modest alternative.

On cross, Brisbin drew attention to the fact that this was new testimony. He asked Miss Scharf if she and Lucinda Kilpatrick had talked about the case together. Miss Scharf replied that they had seen each other often since the funeral and did talk about it. Not only that, but Miss Scharf was now living with the Kilpatricks.

Multiple witnesses close to the Bilanskys testified about Mrs. Bilansky visiting John Walker at night. Dr. Potts testified, as he had at the inquest, that the inflammation in the digestive tract was consistent with arsenic poisoning. Attorney Brisbin extracted a concession from him that it was possible that this had been caused by alcohol abuse, chronic health problems or overuse of patent medicines. Dr. Morton, who also testified, had taken the sample of the digestive tract to a lab in Chicago, owing to inadequate resources for testing in St. Paul. He was satisfied that there was arsenic present. He had also tested one of the dead man's patent medicines and concluded that it contained no harmful ingredients.

This was damning evidence, and the press made much of it.[116] Reporters had predicted that this would be an exciting trial. As the historian Walter Trenerry explained, "The case had created a sensation in St. Paul, which rarely had the treat of finding out how a pretty woman managed to carry on a liaison with a young lover under her elderly husband's very roof."[117] Thus, the defense's cross-examination of Dr. Morton did not have the impact that it deserved. Morton was forced to admit that, of six possible tests for the presence of arsenic, he had declined to attempt one of them, and of those that he had performed, two were unreliable and two did *not* indicate arsenic. That left one positive test result, with nothing to corroborate it. He was also brought to concede that the two boxes of patent medicine, if taken in one dose, would have been fatal. It was Dr. Morton himself who had sold Mr. Bilansky the boxes.

The prosecution rested on Friday, May 28. Brisbin was ill, but Judge Palmer pushed forward. Mr. Williams, co-counsel for the defense, took the lead. His first witness was Ellen Truett, Mr. Bilansky's second wife. She testified that her ex-husband had been a drunk and also depressed, with a morbid fascination with death. He had long harbored a conviction that he would die in March, any March, of any year, based on the fact that his sister had died in March. In February of each year, he would fall into melancholia, preoccupied with what he believed to be his impending demise. Truett said that Ann Bilansky grieved at her husband's funeral and wept on the way home from the burial. This testimony contradicted that given by Lucinda Kilpatrick and Rosa Scharf.

A total of four defense witnesses testified that there were rats in the Bilansky home and that Mr. Bilansky had given away the cat that had been controlling the rat infestation. Four other witnesses testified that Mr. Bilansky had had terrible financial difficulties, and one of them even said that he repeatedly stated that he would rather be dead than alive.

Court adjourned, resuming on Tuesday, May 31. The defense called St. Paul city physician Joseph A. Vervais. Dr. Vervais was dissatisfied with every analysis that had been conducted in the Bilansky case and did not believe that there was sufficient evidence to conclude that there was arsenic in Stanislaus Bilansky's system.

John Walker, on the stand, defended Mrs. Bilansky's virtue. She really was his aunt, he said, and, not only had there been no affair between himself and Mrs. Bilansky, but she had also struck him as a good wife to Stanislaus. Walker may have been telling the truth about her being an aunt, if she were an aunt by marriage, or if they had been committing incest, but it is unlikely that they were not having an affair.

The trial drew to a close on June 10. Judge Palmer charged the jury, and deliberations started at 12:30 p.m. At 5:30 p.m., the jurors came back. The courtroom waited in silence for the verdict: guilty. A jury poll demonstrated that it was a unanimous verdict.

The court denied the defense's motions for a new trial and stay of judgment on June 22. About a week later, Judge Palmer changed his mind and certified the case for review by the Minnesota Supreme Court. Attorney Brisbin, appearing there on July 8, faced the state's first justices of the supreme court: Lafayette Emmett, Isaac Atwater and Charles E. Flandrau. Brisbin argued that his client should be exempt from capital punishment because she was a woman and could read, basing this on an archaic artifact of English common law. In an even more desperate attempt to evade the death penalty, Brisbin argued that English medieval law considered the killing of a husband by a wife to be an act of petty treason, a crime that had been abolished in Minnesota; ergo, the death penalty was abolished *for* it. This, of course, was grasping at straws and did not sway the court. Brisbin's next argument was that Judge Palmer, by permitting Lucinda Kilpatrick to refrain from answering his questions, had interfered with his ability to present his case. The justices of the supreme court disagreed on this point as well.

Flandrau, writing the opinion, explained that there was precedence for dispensing with those particular quirks of English common law and medieval law and also that, as adultery was illegal in Minnesota, Lucinda Kilpatrick could not have been compelled to incriminate herself by admitting to an affair with John Walker. Furthermore, said Flandrau, Judge Palmer had discretion to shut down lines of questioning intended to humiliate a witness. Finally, Brisbin had not proved to the supreme court's satisfaction that Mrs. Kilpatrick admitting to such an affair would have

Portrait of Judge Charles Flandrau, St. Paul, Minnesota. *Nicollet County Historical Society.*

been proof that she had falsely incriminated Mrs. Bilansky.

On hearing the news of the remand for sentencing on July 25, Mrs. Bilansky escaped from jail. This was hardly an act of derring-do. She simply walked out while the jailer was in another building, leaving her unattended in the corridor outside of her cell. About a dozen prisoners had escaped from Ramsey County Jail in a similar manner over the previous three years. The jailer liked Mrs. Bilansky and enjoyed her company, and that was enough to make him trust her to her own devices.

Mrs. Bilansky hid near Lake Como. She managed to get word to Walker. He brought food and a man's outfit for her to wear to disguise herself. On the evening of August 1, they set out for St. Anthony. Deputy Sheriff Turnbull and Officer Church of the St. Paul Police Department overtook them, and they were both brought to Ramsey County Jail. Walker was released within six weeks. Mrs. Bilansky remained incarcerated for the rest of her life.

Willis A. Gorman, former governor and head-basher, was now a practicing attorney. He replaced Brisbin as defense counsel. At the sentencing on December 2, Mrs. Bilansky spoke: "If I die in this case, I die an innocent woman. I don't think I have had a fair and just trial." Judge Palmer informed her that she should not expect a pardon and that the hanging was unavoidable. Mrs. Bilansky wept aloud as the judge sentenced her to a month in solitary confinement, with hanging to follow "at such time as the Governor of this State shall by his warrant appoint."[118]

To hang a woman was a shocking matter. The only person so far who had been judicially hanged in Minnesota was Yu-ha-zee six years earlier. Mrs. Bilansky would be the first person hanged post-statehood. Protests demanding that Sibley, who was now governor, commute her sentence came from strange quarters, and the strangest of them all was Justice Flandrau, who, although he believed that Mrs. Bilansky was guilty, was horrified at the prospect of subjecting a woman to the death penalty. The case led many reformers to oppose capital punishment. On December 13, the judiciary committee of the Minnesota House of Representatives was instructed to look into abolishment of the death penalty in Minnesota. It ultimately decided against taking action.

On January 1, 1860, Alexander Ramsey returned to the governorship. Sibley had declined to sign Mrs. Bilansky's execution warrant, thereby kicking the can down the road to him.

Rosa Scharf was found dead. At the coroner's inquest, it came out that, a few days before her death, she had bought a vial of "unusually strong" laudanum.[119] The empty vial was found in her room. Mr. and Mrs. Kilpatrick testified that she had been with them earlier that evening. Mrs. Kilpatrick said that Rosa had not been acting strangely, but Mr. Kilpatrick said that she had asked about what would happen to Ann Bilansky.

Two weeks after that, Governor Ramsey issued a warrant for Mrs. Bilansky's execution, to take place on March 23. Petitions in support of commutation continued to pour in, but Ramsey was unswayed. The historian Matthew Cecil suggests three reasons for this. First, Ramsey might have been persuaded of her guilt by his brother, Justus Ramsey, who had served on the jury. Second, he could have been willing to sacrifice Mrs. Bilansky's life to spite Mr. Gorman, a political rival for whom he felt no affection whatsoever. Third, commutation might have generated a greater controversy, which was "something a low-key land speculator and veteran politician like Ramsey was trained to avoid."[120]

For nearly a month, between February 10 and March 5, the legislature debated off and on over a commutation bill for the sentence of Mrs. Bilansky. Its sponsors stated that she had not had a fair trial and that it was unappealing to them for the first person executed in the state to be a woman. They passed the bill but Ramsey issued what the *Pioneer and Democrat* described as a "manly veto."[121]

Gorman, Brisbin and even Heard petitioned the governor for commutation on various grounds: the lack of clarity in the arsenic analyses' results; the stated dissatisfaction of two jurors who were second-guessing themselves; the newspapers' vitriolic reporting had spread prejudice against Ann Bilansky; Brisbin's illness during the trial; Gorman himself sincerely believed in her innocence; Brisbin had more evidence that might have been introduced showing that Mr. Bilansky had tried to poison himself years earlier in a failed suicide attempt, which could indicate that this was no murder, but a suicide. All to no avail.

On March 22, Mrs. Bilansky's friends and supporters came to say their final goodbyes. John Walker was not among them. He had left town.

In Court House Square at Cedar and Fifth Streets, a crowd of between 1,500 and 2,000 men, women and children gathered on the midmorning of March 23 to watch the execution. They perched on stone piles, roofs and everywhere with an elevation. At 10:00 a.m., Captain Chamblin of the Pioneer Guard marched into the square. He and his men, all armed, were dressed in overcoats and fatigue caps. They drove the crowd back from the fence and then formed a row of sentinels twenty feet out from the enclosure in front of the courthouse, which filled up the whole block hemmed by Wabasha, Cedar, Fourth and Fifth Streets. Wabasha Street was packed with carriages, wagons and other vehicles on top of which their owners sat for a view, as if it were a drive-in movie theater.

The crowd was mostly composed of immigrants, primarily from Germany and Ireland. There were some native-born St. Paulites and St. Antonians. On a large stone pile in the square sat six Sioux women and their children. "They were evidently interested in the manner the whites dealt out justice to murderers," said the *Pioneer and Democrat*, adding glumly, "We are doubtful if it impressed them with a very forcible idea of our superior civilization."[122]

The jail door opened, and the procession stepped out into the yard: first, Sheriff A.W. Tullis; then the two attending physicians, Dr. Samuel Willey and the Minnesota state surgeon general Dr. Jacob H. Stewart; the Sisters of Charity and two other women; Mrs. Bilansky with a priest and a county official; and finally, fifteen or twenty men who happened to be in the building and who now, apparently, had a front-row seat to an execution. As for the other spectators, they were held at bay by the Pioneer Guard and kept outside an enclosure fence. About one hundred people were present, with permission, inside the fence, but a number of women, perhaps as many as thirty, managed to slip in as well. Some of them had babes in arms, who cried and fussed for the duration of the hanging ritual.

Mrs. Bilansky and her entourage climbed the stairs onto the gallows, next to which a black coffin lay. She knelt at the drop while the others knelt near her, and the priest prayed aloud for several minutes. Then the doomed woman declaimed to the crowd:

> *I die without having any mercy shown me, or justice. I die for the good of my soul, and not for murder. May you all profit by my death. Your courts of justice are not courts of justice—but I will yet get justice in Heaven. I am a guilty woman, I know, but not of this murder....I forgive every body*

who did me wrong. I die a sacrifice to the law. I hope you all may be judged better than I have been, and by a more righteous judge. I die prepared to meet my God. [123]

The sheriff's deputy put the rope around her neck and a black cap over her head.

The last words that Mary Ann Evans Bilansky ever spoke were, "Lord Jesus Christ receive my soul."[124] She was asked to step forward.

Sheriff Tullis triggered the drop. His victim jerked down four feet. "The machinery was so nicely adjusted," reported the *Pioneer and Democrat* approvingly, "that the noise was scarcely heard outside of the enclosure." Mrs. Bilansky convulsed once, and her chest heaved, and then she was forever still. The priest and the nuns knelt in prayer for another twenty minutes. The physicians examined the body several times and then told the sheriff that she was certifiably dead. Her body was taken down and placed in the coffin. Mrs. Bilansky had exhibited remarkable composure at the gallows. It was widely believed that she had "expected a pardon or reprieve to the last moment."[125]

The crowd broke into the courtyard and fought for scraps of rope for souvenirs or for what they believed would be its healing properties, in keeping with old superstitions.

The *Stillwater Messenger*'s correspondent was disgusted by the crowd's behavior at the execution and by the very concept of the death penalty. He could not help but wonder:

Did Mrs. Bilansky speak the truth, in this last awful moment? None but Jehovah will ever know. If she did utter words of truth—if she was innocent of the crime for which she died, there is a terrible responsibility somewhere. If she was innocent, happy is the citizen who has washed his hands of her blood. [126]

11
THE OTHER MURDERS

For years to come, it would aggravate the broad-minded men and women among the St. Paulites that the only people hanged so far in their city had been Yu-ha-zee, whom they saw as vulnerable on account of his race and circumstances, and Mrs. Bilansky, whom they saw as vulnerable on account of her gender. Mrs. Bilansky's hanging was downright bewildering, given the recent fates of other people tried for murder.

In October 1858, five months before Stanislaus Bilansky died, two men gleefully beat the elderly James McClay to death near the corner of Fifth and Minnesota Streets. They were convicted but received no sentence, due to a legal technicality. In January 1859, the body of Mrs. Lawrence Laliyer was found under an icehouse in Mounds View Township, also in Ramsey County. Mr. Laliyer was tried twice for first-degree murder. The second time around, he was convicted of murder in the second degree and given a short prison sentence. On January 26, 1860, Mrs. William O'Neill's body was found at her home in a swamp area by Seventh and Cedar Streets. The autopsy could not determine if it was an accidental death or if Mr. O'Neill had murdered her "in a drunken fit."[127] He was tried, convicted and sentenced to five years in prison.

If these other four killers had been convicted of first-degree murder, then Governor Ramsey almost certainly would have signed their execution warrants. As the next few years would show, he had no aversion to hangings.

12

A GLOOM OVER THE CITY

T he financial destruction of 1857 was still wreaking havoc on St. Paul in the first three years of the 1860s. On top of that, everyone in the country knew that civil war was brewing. In Washington, D.C., Senator Henry M. Rice was hard at work appeasing his colleagues from the South, believing that their secession would be the worst possible outcome. The minute that Rebel soldiers fired on Fort Sumter, he changed his tune and went full throttle for the Northern war effort. St. Paul had little difficulty meeting its draft quotas, owing to both genuine patriotism and the shoddy local economy. Young men were eager to serve and eager for the income, and yet "not only the Civil War but general business conditions cast a gloom over the whole community."[128]

Everyone was on edge. The regulators of public order were no exception. Officers of the court and law enforcement officers alike came to blows with their colleagues. The entire St. Paul police force was demoralized, and 75 percent of the department enlisted in the army. An SPPD publication later characterized this as a desertion, but those men were the smart ones. "The treasury of the city was depleting and one of the worst cris[e]s in the history of the city was the result."[129] Public faith in the remaining 14 officers was so low that in May, Mayor John S. Prince suggested to the city council that it disband the police force. The council compromised, dismissing 7 men. Prince formed a vigilance committee to cover the loss. The vigilance volunteer force consisted of 200 young men. Such citizens as Isaac Heard and his fellow attorney Harvey Officer and the banker Ferdinand Willius numbered among its captains and lieutenants. They would have their work cut out for them that year, keeping order in an anxious city. But the future held something worse: a war much closer to home.

13
BLOOD BOILED

W ho Is to Blame!" raged a front-page headline in the September 11, 1862 issue of the *Saint Paul Daily Press*. "We are in the midst of a struggle with a wily and remorseless foe, accompanied with deeds of horror and attrocity [*sic*] heretofore unknown." The journalist was referring to the Dakota massacre of white settlers that had begun at the Lower Sioux Agency, about one hundred miles southwest of St. Paul. The massacre would last for forty days and leave (an estimated) 358 murder victims. "The hoarded vengeance of an injured, oppressed and defrauded people has at length burst upon our defenseless settlements; and the terrible retribution for a thousand outrages is meted out with indiscriminate hate alike upon the guilty and the innocent."

For those innocents, the *Daily Press* had nothing but compassion. "Our blood curdles in our veins as we read of hearthstones made desolate, infants torn from their mother's breasts, women outraged and violated, millions of property destroyed, unoffending settlers driven from their happy homes, or led to a hopeless captivity." This was horrifying, but it was not mysterious. After all, "Have we never heard of the long series of outrages which prompted these avenging blows?"[130]

The Dakotas had many grievances. The traders were making profits of between 100 and 400 percent on sales to Natives in the 1850s and early '60s, with the collusion of Indian agents. The current agent for the Dakotas, Thomas J. Galbraith, was a lawyer who had served in the Minnesota legislature. He was so proud of his swindle as an Indian agent that he bragged about it to a colleague.[131]

The Dakota War dominated the front page of the *Saint Paul Daily Press* for August 28, 1862 *Minnesota Historical Society, Minnesota Digital Newspaper Hub.*

THE SAINT PAUL DAILY PRESS.

VOLUME II.   SAINT PAUL, SATURDAY, AUGUST 30, 1862.   NUMBER 128.

The Dakota War dominated the front page of the *Saint Paul Daily Press* for August 30, 1862. *Minnesota Historical Society, Digital Newspaper Hub.*

In 1858, Joseph R. Brown, who was at that time an Indian agent, had accompanied Dakota leaders to Washington, D.C., to negotiate more land cessions. When His Scarlet Nation engaged in a flight of oratory that would not have been out of place within a council of fellow Natives, Commissioner Charles E. Mix told the forty-eight-year-old chief that he was acting like a child, threatened to leave and later implied that His Scarlet Nation was unintelligent. Regardless, the Dakotas ceded all their land north of the Minnesota River, nearly one million acres, to the United States. This left them with a ludicrous remnant, 140 miles long and only 10 miles wide, and they would have two agencies, the Upper Sioux Agency and the Lower Sioux Agency. The treaty left open to the Senate "the compensation [the Dakotas] should receive."[132] Brown stated that $5.00 per acre would be a fair value. It was not until June 19, 1860, that the Committee on Indian Affairs concluded that a price of $1.25 per acre would be fitting. On June 27, the committee chairman surreptitiously changed the price to $0.30 per acre. It was the penultimate day of session, and the senators were tired and bored and claimed they didn't even understand the subject. They put off debate on the appropriations for land payment until the next session. "Patient reader," said William W. Folwell in his account of this saga, "do you wonder that Indian blood boiled?"[133] The next year, the annuity payment process was a debacle, as federal officials had made unilateral decisions about the method of payment that did not conform to precedent or expectations.

To give a bare summary of the conditions of the Dakotas the year after that, in summer 1862: they were hungry, the traders would not give them food on credit against their annuity payment, and the payment was late. They had all thought that it would come in mid-July, but as of Sunday, August 17, their money still had not been brought to them. His Scarlet Nation went to church at the Lower Sioux Indian Agency, where he smiled and shook hands with his fellow parishioners. At noon the following day, the keg of gold for the annuity payment arrived at Fort Ridgely seventeen miles from the agency, "by which hour some hundred white people lay in or about their homes dead or bleeding from wounds."[134] His Scarlet Nation, under the influence of Chief Shakopee, led the warriors of the Dakota Uprising.

IF HIS SCARLET NATION were to succeed in subduing the soldiers at Fort Ridgely, then he and his men would have a clear path to the capital city. St. Paulites were in a frenzy of fear. Every day, more refugees staggered into the city with tales of mass murder and rape. Deranged with grief and terror, they misremembered such details as the number of the dead, inflating it in their minds, and also exaggerating the frequency of a very small number of sadistic acts, further frightening the people of St. Paul. As the assorted politicians and businessmen whom Ramsey had appointed to be army officers in the Dakota War in lieu of the real officers fighting in the Civil War rode into the deserted settler villages and towns with their soldiers, they had only to see the evidence of the bodies to know that too many of the stories were true. Justice Flandrau, himself a former Indian agent, was made a colonel and led the Second Battle of New Ulm, where fifty-four settlers had been slaughtered before the army's arrival.

Ramsey requested that his favorite rival, Sibley, serve as colonel. Sibley had no prior military experience, but he would fight in the Dakota War until 1866 and retire a brevet major general. What he saw of the carnage in deserted villages sickened him and gave him a thirst for vengeance.

BACK IN ST. PAUL, the city dwellers weren't frightened only of the Dakotas. For similar reasons, though on a less dire scale, the Ojibwes at their reservations up north were planning their own uprising. Their agent, Lucius C. Walker, three miles outside of Crow Wing County, sent word to nearby Fort Ripley (not to be confused with Fort Ridgely) to have soldiers come to arrest Hole in the Day. Walker had received word that the chief planned to "clean out the country and drive on to St. Paul." The soldiers arrived and would have given chase, but the chief and his wives and children fled to the riverside and climbed into a boat. They had nearly crossed to the west bank of the Mississippi when the soldiers fired at him. He fired back and "henceforth began to incite an uprising in earnest— sending messages of war to all the Chippewa bands as far north as Lake Superior."[135] This kicked off what came to be known as the "Chippewa Disturbance." Walker and his wife escaped to St. Cloud. He sent her off to St. Anthony on August 20. A few days later, Walker was found dead with a bullet in his skull and a revolver lying under his body with one barrel empty. It was assumed that he had killed himself.

Walker had come highly recommended to President Abraham Lincoln for the position of Indian agent, receiving a glowing letter of support from Alexander Ramsey. Walker was also a swindler, and Hole in the Day had had the evidence of financial records to prove it. In June 1862, he took this to William P. Dole, the current commissioner of Indian Affairs. Hole in the Day left Washington, D.C., satisfied that Commissioner Dole, a more respectful man than Mix, would do something about it. Not long after that, Judge David Cooper, Hole in the Day's atorney, announced that the Minnesota senators and congressmen in D.C. had interfered with the investigation into Walker's malfeasance, and it was dead in the water. When Walker died, too, it came as a relief to the Ojibwes.

Meanwhile, in St. Paul, where anyone following the news would have been aware of some or all of this disgraceful treatment and would have known that the Ojibwes had grounds for resentment, even reasonable people trembled at the thought of a massacre from that front as well. Thomas M. Newson, who was living in temporary retirement by Lake Como in Rose Township, in a neighborhood that would soon be annexed by St. Paul, wrote a letter to the editor for the *Daily Press*, printed on August 30:

> *For the past week, the citizens of Rose township…have been excited by information which has been communicated to them by whole families of fugitives, who had left their farms and were fleeing from what they supposed to be the near approach of the tomahawk and the scalping knife of the Chippewas; that a large body of Indians were at and around Rice Lake and a few miles beyond, preparing to pounce upon the defenseless settlers without a moment's warning. The feeling of alarm spread like a contagion, and several families in this town were preparing to move into the city, when a party of gentlemen volunteered to act as scouts, and ascertain, if possible, if such a body of Indians really did exist.*

There are many Rice Lakes in Minnesota, but Newson was likely referring to the one in present-day Lino Lakes, about fourteen and a half miles north of Lake Como.

Newson, whom Hole in the Day had once called a friend, armed himself and rode out on horseback with his neighbors to reconnoiter. At Lake Johanna, in Arden Hills, only one family out of an entire community was left. The others had already moved to St. Paul out of fear of Ojibwes. The remaining family was getting ready to do the same.

In Mounds View Township, a tiny settlement at the time, there were only twenty-seven resident families. On that day, the Lake Como party found only two inhabited houses. The rest of the community had moved, abandoning homes, furnishings, livestock and their unharvested crops.

One of those two remaining residents, Mr. Grant, had sent his family and belongings to St. Anthony. He told Newson that there were 325 Ojibwe warriors near Typo Lake and "that most of them were mounted and well armed; that they were in the habit of alarming the settlers at midnight, and impudently demanding something to eat; that in several instances they had said to the whites that they did not wish to hurt them, but they would *advise them to leave*" (emphasis in original). Typo Lake is thirty-five miles from Lake Como.

Newson and company continued on their journey. Along the way, they saw more signs of deserted settlements. As they neared their destination, "Our mounted men [kept] a sharp look out for the skulking devils, who were reported to be quite near, and soon were at Rice Lake." There, a white family reported that there was an Ojibwe camp in the area consisting entirely of men who did not hunt or fish. They "annoy[ed]…the farmers by their insolence and constant demands for food. Most of the families twenty miles above Rice Lake had moved, and "fears were entertained of an outbreak at any moment."

Newson and his companions rode around the lake, where they found "nearly every house vacated, excepted, perhaps, a man or two…to guard it." A German immigrant who had sent his family to St. Paul told them that he had seen "three Indians traveling across the marsh near his house, and that they were not friendly Indians, as they would neither speak or enter any of the houses." Note that the settlers did not like it when the Natives approached them but also did not like it when the Natives did not approach them. They had been primed by their agitation to see all Natives, doing anything, as a threat. The German concluded that these three Indians were spies, "as their whole conduct was of a suspicious character." His neighbor "corroborated this story, and was satisfied that the Indians were on a mission of evil."

The investigators returned home,

> *fully impressed with these convictions:*
> *1st. There are Chippewa Indians within 40 miles of St. Paul, who have hostile intentions.*
> *2d. That a section of county covering 25 miles, has been almost deserted in consequence of this impression.*
> *3d. That while there may be no immediate danger to either the settlers or the city, yet precautionary measures should at once be taken to kill any Indians who may attempt to commit any outrage upon the whites.*

They held a community meeting. Rose Township formed a home guard, and Newson recommended that St. Paul join them. "We do not propose to forsake our property, but we do propose to kill any hostile, skulking devil who comes across our path."[136]

It must have been a terrifying time to be a Native person in Minnesota. Governor Ramsey, on September 9, expressed what Folwell would recall as a "unanimous sentiment" when he called for the genocide or removal of Dakotas from Minnesota, and what's more, said Folwell, all the newspapers were united in extending this "sentiment" to include "every Indian of every tribe in the state."[137] This included the Ho-Chunk, who had caused no harm to either soldiers or civilians. This completely innocent community was soon driven from Minnesota by force. A company of soldiers was stationed at Anoka to protect St. Paul from a possible attack by Ojibwes.

In the end, the "Disturbance" was brief and bloodless. Hole in the Day made peace with the United States. The Ojibwes were not removed from Minnesota, and Ojibwe warriors allied with U.S. soldiers against the Dakotas.

His Scarlet Nation did not participate in the massacres. He had wanted to fight a white man's war and focused his strategy on soldier-to-soldier conflict. His warriors fought hard. In one battle alone, at Birch Coulee in Renville County, twenty-three St. Paul men died and forty-five suffered nonfatal wounds. However, the raids on settlers depleted his ranks, as a man could not be in two places at once. The men who committed massacres cost the Dakota army its victory. If His Scarlet Nation "could have led his warriors against [Fort Ridgely] [sooner], they might have made an easy capture," but "his young men in considerable numbers were widely dispersed, engaged in carnage and plunder....The delay gave opportunity for reënforcing the garrison."[138]

Sibley not only managed to secure the release of settlers whom the Dakotas had taken prisoner, but he also oversaw the surrender of approximately 2,000 people. He ordered that they be sorted into combatants and noncombatants. When that was done, the 1,658 noncombatants, mostly women, children and elderly people, were brought to Fort Snelling in November and held in a concentration camp at the river bottom below the fort. They were forced to perform strenuous and unpleasant labor, such as burying horse carcasses. They were poorly fed, at least one woman was gang-raped by soldiers and conditions were unsanitary. Measles, to which Dakotas had little immunity, ravaged the camp, as did other illnesses. Somewhere between 130 and 300 people died there that winter.[139]

To Sibley's horror, army officers, and then Governor Ramsey, set bounties for the scalps of "Sioux warriors," an incentive to murder any Native man on sight. At one point, Ramsey's bounty was as high as $200 per scalp.

Throughout the month of October, a military commission guided by Isaac Heard, who performed the duties of a judge advocate (though officially a recorder), had tried 392 men for their actions in the Dakota War. Each case was slammed through in a matter of minutes, and 303 men were given a death sentence. President Lincoln was flooded with petitions to hang them all. Ramsey sent him badgering telegrams to advance the cause of hanging them—and hanging them *now*. A rumor had circulated that Lincoln would not allow the condemned men to be executed. In response, 300 St. Paulites convened at a community meeting to draft a memorial:

> *To the President of the United States:*
>
> *We, the citizens of Saint Paul…have heard…reports of an intention…to dismiss without punishment, the Sioux warriors captured by our soldiers; and further, to allow the several tribes of Indians lately located upon reservations within this State, to remain upon the reservations….*
>
> *These facts have made the question simply whether the Indians or the white race shall possess Minnesota. What immigrant will bring his family to a land where the savages are in such close proximity, that he is liable any day to be shot…or on his return home from his day's labor to find his family outraged and murdered?*
>
> *Minnesota is the best farming State in the Union.…It is capable of sustaining a purely agricultural population of millions, and in addition possesses great facilities for manufacturing.…Shall we…be driven into exile by the savages[?]…*
>
> *[W]e demand that the captive Indians…proved before a military commission…shall receive the punishment due those crimes.…*
>
> *We ask further that these savages may be removed from close proximity to our settlements.…*
>
> *We hope that men whose friends and relations have been foully murdered by these Indian devils, will not be compelled to take vengeance into their own hands, as they assuredly will if Government shall fail in its duty in the matter.[140]*

Unstated in that final sentence, but made explicit in a communication from Sibley's superior, Brigadier General John Pope, was that the targets of the vengeance would be the innocent prisoners at the Fort Snelling camp. This was a credible threat. When the prisoners, under military escort, were on their way to Fort Snelling, settler mobs had had to be driven back with bayonets. Lieutenant Colonel William R. Marshall, a co-owner of the *St. Paul Daily Press*, directed the march and did everything in his power to prevent violence. But on one occasion, Samuel J. Brown, son of Joseph R. Brown, saw a white woman break past the military guard, snatch a nursing Dakota infant from a mother's breast and "dash it violently upon the ground." Soldiers "dragged" the white woman away and brought the baby back to its mother, but it was too late. The battered infant died within a few hours.[141]

Lincoln ordered a reexamination of trial records, this time focused on identifying those men who had committed rape or murder of noncombatant settlers, as opposed to those who had only fought against Minnesotan soldiers under His Scarlet Nation. The task was assigned to Joseph R. Brown. One of the men he identified was a Black man married into a Dakota family who had been forced to participate in the massacres and had enthusiastically cooperated with the military commission. His sentence was commuted to ten years in prison. One man was respited. Two other men, Shakopee and Medicine Bottle, escaped to Canada, thus evading trial, but they had committed capital offenses.

Thirty-eight Dakotas were hanged in Mankato on December 26, 1862. Among them were several men who had had nothing to do with the massacres and were sentenced in error.

The following year, an act of Congress abrogated all treaties with the Dakotas, rendering them landless, as Ramsey had so long desired. A second act provided for their removal from state borders. Lincoln chose a spot on the Missouri River, not far from Fort Randall. The noncombatants in the Fort Snelling camp would be sent there first. As they assembled at the levee on May 4, St. Paulites taunted them and threw stones. They all made it intact to the Missouri River, but the boat to which they transferred was overcrowded. "There was not room enough for all to lie down at night and they were forced to sleep by relays. The weather was already hot and the rations…were musty." It took weeks of the boat's laboring against the powerful river current before they arrived on May 30. They did not all survive those conditions, and "as a result…the hills about Crow Creek were soon covered with graves."[142]

This was not the entire population of Dakota noncombatants. In Sibley's initial campaign, he and his men had halted their pursuit at the shore of the Missouri River. Dakota warriors had held the soldiers at bay so that the women, children, the infirm and the elderly advancing ahead of them could escape across the river. Only then did the warriors who could get away follow them. There would be later campaigns to drive them farther away, but at least they had saved themselves and their loved ones from imprisonment.

The Fort Snelling camp would only briefly be empty. The warriors who had received prison sentences instead of death sentences had been kept at Mankato, but in 1863, they were brought to other military installations, including Fort Snelling, and were later pardoned before being transported from the state. The annuity payments restarted, despite the abrogation. There were still isolated Dakota attacks on settlers who had remained or returned. There was a raid on June 29, 1863, not far from St. Paul, and another on July 1 in Wright County. Two days after that, Nathan Lampson and his son Chauncey saw two Native men picking berries in a thicket in McLeod County. The Lampsons, who were armed, ambushed the Natives and murdered one of them, but the other got away. The murder victim's body was thrown in an offal pit. The one who escaped, a boy of sixteen, was later arrested. It was his father who had been murdered. His father was His Scarlet Nation. Their leader was dead, but his men fought on as best they could. Then, in January 1864, nearly one hundred Dakota warriors surrendered.

THE MINNESOTA MILITARY AUTHORITIES were determined to get their hands on Medicine Bottle and Shakopee. The latter was the true instigator. He had had a good reason for it: a gang of young men from his village had impulsively killed a farmer and his family, and Shakopee knew that the settlers and the State of Minnesota were looking for an excuse to get rid of the Dakotas. They could either rally or be slaughtered. The conditions were ripe for an outbreak of mass violence.

In April 1864, Shakopee and Medicine Bottle were located in Canada, drugged, bound and brought to Fort Snelling for trial. The two men were found guilty of murdering multiple white people, one of whom was Philander Prescott, the fur trader whose false statement had led to Agent Taliaferro's arrest back in 1839. A reporter who attended Shakopee and Medicine Bottle's trials was dissatisfied and believed that they had been convicted on the basis of evidence that would not have sufficed to convict a white man.[143] After the trial, the two warriors waited, imprisoned at the fort,

THE BUILDING UP OF

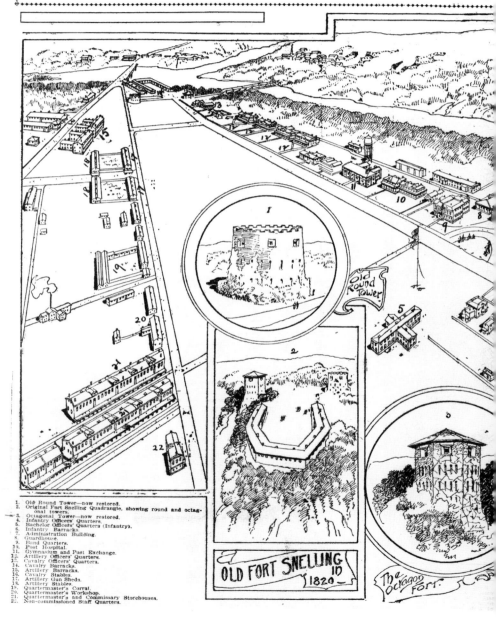

1. Old Round Tower—now restored.
2. Original Fort Snelling Quadrangle, showing round and octagonal towers.
3. Octagonal Tower—now restored.
4. Infantry Officers' Quarters.
5. Bachelor Officers' Quarters (Infantry).
6. Infantry Barracks.
7. Administration Building.
8. Guardhouse.
9. Band Quarters.
10. Post Hospital.
11. Gymnasium and Post Exchange.
12. Artillery Officers' Quarters.
13. Cavalry Officers' Quarters.
14. Cavalry Barracks.
15. Artillery Barracks.
16. Cavalry Stables.
17. Artillery Gun Sheds.
18. Artillery Stables.
19. Quartermaster's Corral.
20. Quartermaster's Workshop.
21. Quartermaster's and Commissary Storehouses.
22. Non-commissioned Staff Quarters.

DITION

RT SNELLING ⚜

"The Building up of Fort Snelling." Much expansion occurred during and after the Dakota War. *Minnesota Historical Society, Minnesota Digital Newspaper Hub.*

Scott, after inspecting rested in his report to the ment, "the propriety of name to Fort Snelling as a ent to the meritorious of- presently sought to recover their free- dom by instituting the suit decided by the federal supreme court. Slaves were once common at Snell- ing, although the only purchaser ment of his claim. it is estimated to have cost him, eventually, about $9 an ore. He obtained among the rest the beautiful valley of Minnehaha creek and the famous falls as well. It was

for more than a year before being executed. The soldiers liked them, as they were cooperative and cheerful.

At their hanging at Fort Snelling on November 11, 1865, Medicine Bottle and Shakopee stood on the scaffold "without the apparent movement of a muscle," having maintained an "astonishing firmness" from the moment they had emerged before more than one thousand spectators. The drop was triggered at noon sharp. Their necks broke as they fell. Shakopee's legs twitched slightly, and then he was still. As for Medicine Bottle, "his strong, muscular frame clung to life with wonderful tenacity. His writhings were pitiful to behold, and nearly ten minutes had elapsed before his struggles ended."[144] Ten minutes after that, they were pronounced dead. The audience stole relics: pieces of the rope, chips of wood cut from the gallows and the dead men's hats. "The curtain falls," wrote the reporter from the *Mankato Union*, "which hides forever the final scene in the bloody drama of the massacre in Minnesota."[145]

To the exasperation of Minnesota's soldiers, it was not over yet. They would not be mustered out until 1866. All of their actions in that remaining time were punitive expeditions. Pope, now a major general, "charged in an official paper that influential citizens were conspiring to prolong the Indian war for the sake of maintaining [a] profitable market."[146] This was no longer Ramsey's war but instead that of current governor Stephen Miller, who had made a name for himself in railroads and mercantile operations. But it was a continuation of Ramsey's project. He had a personal incentive to reassure land buyers that the Dakotas were far away from Minnesota, that the state government was strong and that it could protect settlers. He had made "large and judicious investments in real estate, which [would] ultimately...become of great value and...the bulk of a comfortable fortune."[147]

In 1867, Joseph R. Brown, with the title of Special Agent, brought leaders of two noncombatant Dakota tribes to Washington, D.C., to have their treaty rights restored and to get a reservation. They were successful, but they were placed outside of Minnesota. In the 1880s, leaders from the tribes that were involved in the war went through a similar process but were allowed to return to the state. They now have four reservations in Minnesota. Their efforts to regain possession of land that was taken from them during the war are ongoing.

PART IV

HORROR ON THE HOMEFRONT

14

THE EXPLODING BOAT

From the spring of 1861 through February 1866, St. Paul continuously had men at war. Their families at home cycled among pride, anxiety, excitement and grief, but war was not all that troubled the community.

November 4, 1864, brought the explosion of the *John Rumsey* steamboat, "[probably] the most terrible accident which ever occurred here."[148] Around three o'clock p.m., the concussion shook city buildings like an earthquake, sending St. Paulites out into the street. The sound had come from the direction of the lower levee, and a crowd formed there frantic for the safety of loved ones involved in the river traffic. They saw an awful sight.

The *Rumsey* and another steamboat, the *Albany*, had been heading up the river. At the bend downriver of St. Paul, the *Albany* was slightly ahead, but the *Rumsey*, a faster boat, drew parallel with it. They were neck and neck at the point where they were just below the levee when the *Rumsey*'s boiler exploded. The vessel caught fire and began to sink. Fifteen minutes later, the fire had destroyed every part of it not already submerged. The *Albany* had also caught fire. Pulling two barges behind it, the vessel slogged up to the levee. The crew of the *Mollie Mohler*, which was at the wharf, steamed over to the *Rumsey* and rescued its surviving crew and barges.

That night, rumors ran through St. Paul, overestimating the number of the dead. It was said that the explosion was caused by irresponsible behavior, that the boats had been racing each other and that this had contributed to the explosion. An inquest later found this false.

Boat docked at the St. Paul Lower Levee at First and Jackson Streets. *Hennepin County Library Digital Collections.*

The explosion threw three of the *Rumsey*'s deckhands onto one of the *Albany*'s barges. They died instantly. Theodore Provencha, the *Albany*'s cook, had stepped from the boat to the barge just before the boiler ruptured and disappeared without a trace. The *Rumsey*'s fireman, John Rothmeyer, also died instantly, and his body went down with the boat. John McCaffray, the *Rumsey*'s second cook, had been out of the immediate range of the explosion, but he was missing. It was assumed that he had leapt into the water to escape and drowned. Another deckhand was blown into the river. While all of their names were known—Michael Melville, Patrick Donovan, Daniel Sweeny and Edward Kearney—it was difficult to put names to faces of the three whose bodies had not been lost, owing to the conditions of the corpses. All but Donovan's body would later be identified. His was believed lost to the river.

Captain Davidson, who owned the *Albany* and was leasing the *Rumsey*, was at the levee. He helped care for the wounded until they were brought, along with the recovered bodies, to St. Joseph's Hospital. There, Dr. Jacob H. Stewart and one of his colleagues tended to the survivors. Michael Melville's sister came to the hospital and was able to identify his body. She "was nearly or quite crazy when she found he was killed."[149] Families of civilian men were not prepared for this.

Some of the survivors' injuries were minor, mere bruising, but other men had broken bones, and one man had nearly gotten his eye cut out. All of the wounded went to stay at the International Hotel, where Davidson paid for their accommodations and visited with them to make sure that they had everything they needed. This might seem very generous of Davidson, but it may have been a manipulative strategy. It took years of litigation to get him to pay out to support the twelve fatherless children and their widowed mothers.[150]

15

THE MOST HORRIBLE SIGHT

On December 19, 1864, the draft was raised, demanding a quota of two hundred men from St. Paul. Charles Stelzer's name was among those chosen, and he appeared before the draft board on Thursday, December 22. The examining physicians determined that his physical disability exempted him from the draft. One of the doctors, who knew him personally, said that he also had dementia.

These impairments did not interfere with his work as a cigar maker and a horse doctor, and he earned a small but steady income. The family could be described as "respectable poor." Their children were well fed and well clothed. A neighbor remembered them as "lively and comfortably cared for."[151] The day before his appearance at the draft board, Charles Stelzer had surprised his wife, Eleanor Baxter Stelzer, with new dresses for herself and their two daughters, Eleanor, age five and a half, and Clotha, who was two years old. For their four-year-old son, William, he got a tiny chair; for Eleanor, a toy table; and for Mrs. Stelzer, a sewing stand. The next morning, feeling irritable, Mrs. Stelzer threw the dresses into the rag box. She asked her husband for ten dollars for traveling money to visit her brother, who lived some ways out of town. Mr. Stelzer asked her to wait a few days so that he could come up with the money.

After getting his exemption, Mr. Stelzer went shopping and bought Christmas presents for the children. He returned home to the single-room apartment in the tenement house they shared with the Cullinane family, across the street from the Summit Avenue House hotel (the site of present-day Summit Overlook Park), which stood at Ramsey Street and Summit.

Mrs. Stelzer asked him to get firewood. He wanted to stay at home, but she told him that bad weather was coming and they would not be able to get it later. Mr. Stelzer left. While he was out on his horse, heading for the Lake Como area, he had the sensation of being blinded with fear that something was wrong at home, and he almost went back.

Around 5:30 p.m., Mr. Stelzer returned. He dismounted, leaving his horse in front of the house. The outside door, as usual, was unlocked. He went into the building and then tried to open the door to his family's apartment. It didn't budge. Mrs. Cullinane was walking by, and she told him that she had seen Mrs. Stelzer a few minutes earlier, although they had only spoken at the door and Mrs. Cullinane had not seen into the room.

Mr. Stelzer forced the door. It had been held closed by a table with chairs wedged between it and one of the two stoves. The curtains were drawn, and the candle was out, but the dying embers in the fireplace partially illuminated the room. The first thing that Mr. Stelzer saw was William, sitting in the large rocking chair. His head was hanging over one side, his brains bulging out of a fracture in his skull. The crown was almost completely cut off from the rest of his head. Mr. Stelzer tried to move him, and some of William's brain matter dropped onto the father's hand. He laid his son on the floor with a pillow under his head. Then he noticed the rest of his family.

Meanwhile, Mrs. Cullinane ran to their neighbor, George W. Penny. He was in the middle of a meal but followed Mrs. Cullinane outside, lighting his lantern. Charles Stelzer came up to him and told him that his wife and children were dead. Together with another neighbor, Mr. Garvin, they went back to the Stelzer apartment.

In the back of the room, on the floor next to the kitchen stove, Mr. Penny saw little Eleanor lying on her side. A hatchet was lying next to her bloodied head. On the other side of the stove lay Mrs. Stelzer. She was on her back with a knife lodged in her neck, blood spurting in jets from the wound. She was still alive, eyes open but unmoving, and she made a gurgling sound in her throat. She was writhing and "turned over partly on her side in her struggles." Mr. Stelzer reached out to remove the knife, but Mr. Penny told him to leave it there, as she was past saving.

Clotha lay on the bed. She looked like she was sleeping. There was a bruise over her left ear. Mr. Stelzer applied a damp rag to her head, and she woke up crying. By the light of his lantern, Mr. Penny examined William and Eleanor more carefully and saw that they were breathing. He went for a doctor and the police.

Dr. Stewart, who had been an attending physician at Mrs. Bilansksy's hanging, served as a surgeon in the Civil War and was now mayor of St. Paul. He arrived around 7:30 p.m. He could do nothing to save Mrs. Stelzer, even as blood continued to leap from her severed carotid artery and jugular vein. She died that evening. The two elder children were also beyond his aid. William moaned in pain. Eleanor rocked side to side in her agony. She could not speak, but her inarticulate vocalizations suggested some degree of consciousness. She was rolled over onto her back, and her brains fell out onto the hatchet beside her. They put a pillow under her head, and she was not moved after that. William was placed next to her. She was dead by 7:45 p.m. William died a few minutes later. Throughout those last hours of his life, he clutched a toy that he had been playing with when he was struck.

The doctor cleaned and dressed Clotha's wound. She was conscious and wept with pain but was able to speak to her father. "My baby," he called her as he tried to comfort her.

That evening, a reporter from the *Saint Paul Press* came into the home. How discordant that human misery was, in the "plain but comfortable" setting. It was a small room, twelve by fifteen feet, but not a bad-looking place at all, aside from the people in it. Mrs. Stelzer had been rolled onto her back and her limbs straightened. The knife was left sticking out of her neck, and her head lay in a pool of blood. "Brains are scattered upon the floor and the blood of the murdered children mingles with the threads of the carpet. Clotha lay on the bed, 'occasionally crying sadly but much of the time in a kind of stupor.'" The reporter concluded, "If a more heart-rending scene can be crowded within twelve by fifteen we hope we shall never be called upon to witness it."[152]

The inquest was a gloomy affair. It was held in the Cullinanes' apartment. Coroner Sheig had given orders to leave the Stelzers' room undisturbed so that his jury could see the evidence. The public were also allowed to view the room, and quite a few people did so.

Despite the crowd, a reporter who had been there the night before felt that it "seemed more desolate than yesterday," as the

cold, dull light of a winter morn shone in at the windows, disclosing even more horrors than the dim rays of a candle had shown the night previous. The pallid, ghastly faces of the dead, distorted and streaked with blood, the glazed, fixed eyes, the hair matted with gore and brains—this made indeed a horrible scene. The floor was covered with blood, brains, and clots of gore, from which a sickening stench arose, as a fire had been kept all night by those who took charge of the place.

The coroner got there at about 10:00 a.m., with a jury of six. Mrs. Cullinane was away, visiting her deathly ill mother in Mendota and presumably brought her children with her.

Charles Stelzer was an immigrant from Germany. He gave testimony in English, his second language. "I had plenty of provisions in the house. I had just bought her and the children dresses and presents, to make her more satisfied." He explained that Mrs. Stelzer's "mind turned" after the death of eight-year-old Laura, the eldest of their four children, from diphtheria. Mrs. Stelzer tried several times to take her own life: once by gunshot, but she did not know how to load the gun, and it misfired; once by poisoning, but she couldn't go through with it; and once by jumping off a bridge, before she realized that she wanted to be with her children. Over the previous two weeks, Mrs. Stelzer would not do any cooking, and Mr. Stelzer hired help for her. The servant had left a few days before the slaughter.

Mrs. Stelzer had had troubles before that, recalled Mr. Stelzer. "She was a hard character when I married her—still I got along with her as well as I could, for the sake of the children. Her brothers and sisters tried to get her to behave herself, but she would not mind them." Mrs. Stelzer was also an immigrant, from England. Her family had come to the United States when she was a child, and they settled in Illinois. Her mother died when she was seven or eight years old. From what Mrs. Stelzer had told him of her mother, Mr. Stelzer believed that she "was a nervous, frettish woman. Any excitement would make her shiver or tremble. She died from fretting." Mr. Baxter, her father, remarried. Her stepmother abused her so badly that she left home and worked in domestic service in both homes and hotels. She was twenty-one years old when she married Charles Stelzer.

In Mr. Stelzer's cigar store, he also sold books, and the young Mrs. Stelzer constantly read murder mysteries and "talked about killing continually. I often tried to stop her talking about it." Her dark impulses manifested in fits of violence. "She used to treat the children cruelly, whipping them severely, before she took this melancholy spell when our little girl died." She would say that she was sorry afterward, but she "seemed not to notice [the children]."

In April, two months after Laura's death, William got sick. Mrs. Stelzer "left him on the floor, so that he should take cold and die." Mr. Stelzer got angry and hit her. "She got down on her knees and promised never to do so again. That was the only time I ever licked her."

At the coroner's request, Charles Stelzer produced the hatchet that was found by his wife's head. He said that it belonged to him and that he had left it in his toolbox. The knife found in his wife's throat was also his. "I had it hid carefully away, as I felt afraid she might use it."

Mr. Penny told the jury that he had at times seen Mrs. Stelzer "rambling around, seemingly melancholy. Her actions would attract attention. I never heard that anybody considered her dangerous." Mrs. Penny said that she had often said to her sister, when she saw Mrs. Stelzer wandering around on the street, that "the woman was out of her mind. She seemed much dejected and sad." Another neighbor said, "I have seen Mrs. Stelzer frequently....She was out of her mind."

Dr. Stewart testified as to what he saw that night. He spoke in dry, precise medicalese as he described the wounds, but then he lost his composure. "*The heads of the children seemed literally chopped to pieces with several blows!...*It was the most horrible sight I ever saw, even in army hospitals!" (emphasis in original).

He had known the family for a while. Mrs. Stelzer came to see him some time after Laura's death. She saw Dr. Stewart's young daughter and "remarked that she reminded her of her lost child. She got quite overcome with sorrow, and cried so much that she could not say a word more, and thus went away." Mr. Stelzer came to Dr. Stewart twice to consult with him about his wife. He described her behavior as "ugly." Dr. Stewart explained to the jury, "I was afraid he would scold and abuse her, and directed him to treat her gently and kindly—and to take her to places of amusement and pleasure, so as to enliven her mind." His theory was that, in her madness, Mrs. Stelzer had hoped to follow Laura in death and to bring the other children with her.

Mr. Stelzer, in the opinion of one reporter, was "a right-meaning and kind-hearted but not very intelligent man, as it seems, [and] unfortunately knew not 'how to minister to a mind diseased.'"[153] Dr. Stewart had not known, either.

Coroner Sheig arranged for the county to provide coffins, as Mr. Stelzer could not afford them. His wife and older children were interred at Oakland Cemetery. Clotha had not fully recovered, and there was still a possibility that she had sustained severe brain damage and even that she might soon die. Mr. Stelzer did not think that he would have enough money to cover her medical bills. The day of the funeral, he gave away his only living child to "some ladies" staying at the Summit House who offered to care for her "until other arrangements can be made for the little sufferer."[154]

16

A SORDID, HOPEFUL CITY

S t. Paul was riding high by the end of the Civil War. True, there had been a stabbing in February 1865, resulting in the prolonged death of the victim, but that was the kind of thing that could happen in any city. The local and state economies were thriving. Not every St. Paulite benefited from it, as there was a "large number" of "destitute families of soldiers," but the citizens who could afford to give to charity had done so, and altogether they donated $225,000 during the war years to "the Sanitary and Christian commissions, to hospital funds and other war charities, to the families of soldiers, and to numerous special cases of distress, &c."[155] The city population swelled to 12,976.

During the spring and summer after the April 9 treaty at Appomattox, Union soldiers returned from the South, to be mustered out at Fort Snelling. Of the St. Paulite men who had gone to war, 8 percent did not return. "Many of them lie in unrecorded graves on battle-fields where they fell, or heaped in the burial-trench of some prison-pen, the victims of disease and starvation."[156] No monument was at that time erected in their honor.

Enthusiasm was the order of the day, as a new "era seemed to have commenced with the close of the [civil] war." The Dakota War troops had yet to be mustered out, but the city was profiting financially from cash infusions from the U.S. government to support ongoing warfare, as Fort Snelling was the base of operations for the punitive expeditions. The papers reported on troop movements as blithely as if the men were going on vacation: "General Sibley received orders yesterday directing him to send Major Brackett's

Battalion to Sioux City, Iowa, without delay....[Major Brackett's] friends will regret to learn that he leaves...next Tuesday. His battalion will be the gainer, however, as he is a favorite with both officers and men."[157]

Scattered accounts appeared in the St. Paul newspapers of violence on the frontier, of whites killing Dakotas and Dakotas killing whites. In May, a St. Paul gun store displayed the severed, as-yet-undecomposed head of Chief Standing Buffalo. It was a grotesque trophy.[158] St. Paulites were well aware that the war went on, but it did not overshadow their mood.

Nor did assorted mayhem: drownings, con artistry, assaults, highway robberies and drunk and disorderly conduct. There were few of any of those cases, and the latter, which was the most common type, sent only one or two people to police court per day. "This court has come to be quite a monotonous institution," the *Saint Paul Press* complained.[159] There was some excitement in late August, when a man's body was found in the river below Dayton's Bluff, so decayed that it was unrecognizable. A rope had been tied around the neck and attached to a stone. After a cursory inquest, the victim was buried in Oakland Cemetery without anyone bothering to make a record of the grave's location. The city forgot about him for the present.

St. Paul was a cheerful place with much to celebrate, on top of the conclusion of the "Slaveholders' Rebellion." Williams recalled, "Our city entered on a career of unusual prosperity. Money was abundant, capital came in from abroad; business never was more flourishing; real estate buoyant; immigration increasing; employment plenty for all classes; every branch of trade and manufacture brisk, and everything presented a vivid contrast to the despondent days from 1857 to 1862."[160]

Isaac Heard, now the St. Paul City Attorney, was not celebrating. There was an element to his new job for which his stint as a prosecuting attorney in the antebellum years had not prepared him: the high rate of postwar juvenile delinquency. This is not a surprising outcome, given the number of families disrupted by war, with fathers and elder brothers returning traumatized or not at all. It would have been stranger if there hadn't been a widespread (if temporary) increase in delinquency. Heard found himself frequently working on cases with child defendants, whose "confessions... were deplorable, and exhibited an amount of depravity...that alarmed [him] and excited his sympathies."[161]

One morning, Heard stepped into the city jail on his way to court to see who had been brought in. He told the story years later, when it had become a part of his personal legend: "In one of the cells were two boys, seven or eight years old, who were crying bitterly. I asked them what was the matter, and found they were frightened at two rats which had come during the night."[162] Children, he resolved, did not belong in city lockups.

Before the year was out, he got the ball rolling on a solution to this problem. He reported to City Hall that there were at least seven youth gangs in St. Paul, with more than two hundred members, many of them under the age of ten. They committed thefts, but what was done to them upon their arrest was worse than what they did: "Let anyone not hardened by crime step into our city prison and see these little children cast shivering and weeping into a prisoner's gloomy cell, and he must say that it is a sin to longer delay action in this matter—a sin that will be visited on the heads of all the people before many years."

He proposed what he called a "House of Refuge," a reform school. "The expense which the city would incur…must be of a small moment in comparison with the salvation of a generation which is now slowly but surely fitting itself for the penitentiary and the gallows."[163]

The reform school opened in 1868, to his joy, but Heard would live long enough to learn that it was no inoculation against the gallows: in 1894, two alumni would be hanged for murder.

17

PAINFUL AS IT IS MYSTERIOUS

I n an otherwise peaceful era in St. Paul, the Van Solen murder trials of 1866 and 1868 "startled the little community at that time, and [were] the talk of the Northwestern country."[164] The *Dodge County Republican* gave its lurid opinion that "the details of the plot show an audacious coolness seldom paralleled in criminal annals."[165]

In the late spring or summer of 1865, the physician Henry Harcourt, who was living in St. Louis, wrote home to friends in England to tell them about his planned trip to Minnesota. He enclosed a letter that he had received in April from W.S. Masters, secretary of a northbound expedition leaving from St. Paul. According to the letter, this expedition required an accompanying surgeon, and Masters invited Harcourt to join them. Masters gave a reference, George L. Van Solen of St. Paul. The letter directed Harcourt to send his reply to post office box 1593. His friends never heard from him again.

After some time, they grew concerned and wrote to Van Solen, inquiring after Harcourt. Van Solen answered their letter and said that he did not know where Harcourt was. With his signature, he wrote, "P.O. Box 1593." The friends then got in touch with the St. Paul authorities. It took direct effort from Chief of Police McIlrath, but they built up enough evidence for an arrest warrant. Van Solen's reputation didn't help. He had, "before entering the army, [been] regarded as an honorable young man," but the war must have changed him. In the time since his homecoming, he had "fallen in the estimation of his friends, many of whom are not surprised at his arrest for this horrible crime." On September 23, 1866, he was picked up in Chicago, where he was working as a hotel night clerk, and brought back to St. Paul.

Van Solen had been the hospital steward of the Sixth Minnesota Infantry, a position requiring a high level of responsibility. During the end of his term of service, he was stationed in St. Louis, where he met Dr. Harcourt, and they became friends. They maintained a correspondence after Van Solen's return to St. Paul.

Harcourt came to St. Paul around August 15 for the expedition, which did not exist. He "is supposed [to have] had with him about $1600."[166] He stayed with Van Solen at his father's home and knew nobody else in the neighborhood. On August 19, the two friends went hunting or fishing in Pig's Eye (now Pig's Eye Regional Park). Harcourt was not seen again.

A day or two after the fishing trip, Van Solen made a complaint with the police against Harcourt. He claimed that the doctor had stolen sixty dollars from him. Van Solen gave them a description of Harcourt that did not in the least resemble him.

A few days later, that decomposed body that no one was able to identify, with a stone tied to it with a rope, washed up below Dayton's Bluff. Now, more than one year later, Drs. Murphy and Wharton, along with Chief McIlrath and Henry J. Horn, Ramsey County Attorney, went together to Oakland Cemetery, where they received the shock that there was no record of the location of the grave. They were in luck, however, as one of the gravediggers who had buried that body remembered where it was.

They exhumed the body. The flesh was gone, but the clothes, including gaiters, were intact, as was the rope around the neck. The doctors examined the skull more carefully and discovered that "*the jaw and part of the skull was found to be shattered by small shot*, evidently fired out of a shot gun!" (emphasis in original).[167] Inside the skull, they found several pellets. At the inquest in August 1865, a juror had noticed that the flesh was gone from the corpse's face, leading Horn and the other three men to believe that the charge of shot had torn off the skin from the victim's face.

That December, Isaac Heard and Cushman K. Davis, a former state legislator, served as Van Solen's defense team for the trial, Judge S.M. Flint presiding. Heard and Davis argued that the body was not Harcourt's and therefore could not be connected to Van Solen. Attorney Horn's evidence that it really was Harcourt was that it matched his build, and also that Dr. Harcourt was known to have worn gaiters. The defense prevailed. The verdict "was not in accord with public sentiment."[168] Even Van Solen's mother believed that her son had murdered Harcourt.

There was a second trial in the late summer of 1868, commencing on July 20. On the evening of August 7, the jury returned a verdict of not guilty, and Van Solen was discharged for good. A reporter reflected that "Van Solen has endured the long imprisonment and the incidents of both trials with great equanimity, and heard the verdict without emotion." Furthermore, "it is a case painful as it is mysterious, and one of the dark riddles that occur more frequently in real-life than on the attractive pages of fiction."[169]

PART V

THE BLOODY FALL

18

A "DEAD TOUGH" TOWN

Aside from the Van Solen trials, the latter half of the 1860s was a time of (imperfect) serenity and prosperity. For a few years after the war, St. Paul continued to receive money from the federal government, which stimulated the local economy. In 1867 alone, 343 buildings were erected.[170] The city grew in those few years without facing the downsides of population increase. It was not innocent of violence, and there were still homicides, but they were few and far between. Come the 1870s, all bets were off.

In 1870, there were 20,030 people in St. Paul. It was the dawn of a new, darker day. The journalist Alix J. Muller wrote in her chronicle of the police and fire departments of St. Paul:

> In the seventies, St. Paul…was known up and down the river as a "dead tough" town. As a matter of evolution and the forming of municipal character this stage of civic existence was perhaps essential to its growth; as a matter of river frontage and inadequate police protection it certainly could not have been much better….Third st. was the main thoroughfare, the principal business street, as well as the most fashionable boulevard at command. But Second, then Bench st., was most popular with such masses as daily sifted into the city; low river dives and dance halls, and groggeries, flourished there, and no respectable man, much less a woman, dared enter the neighborhood after dark. Not a house on the Second Ward front but had its record of crime and vice; in one the gang of sharpers lying in wait for the

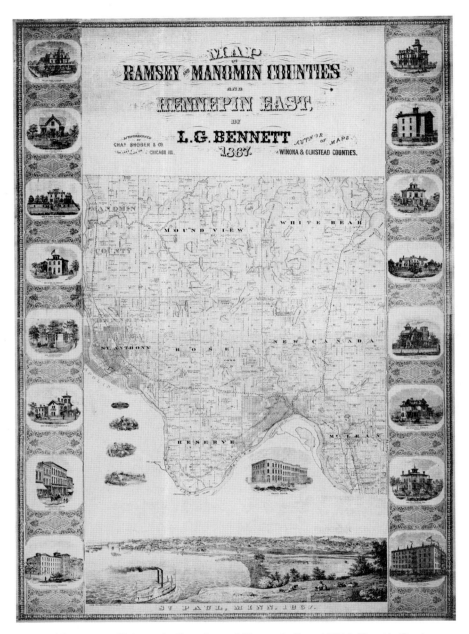

"Map of Ramsey and Manomin Counties and Hennepin East, 1867." *Hennepin County Library Digital Collections.*

"Corner of Jackson Street and 4th Street, Looking Toward 5th Street," 1875. *Hennepin County Library Digital Collections.*

approach of a "tenderfoot," in the other the relay of frail and tawdy [sic] *women, ready to murder the souls of men, and in yet another the vender of distilled poison.*[171]

This was not simply the way things were for cities at that time. While vice had a heyday in the region, St. Paul was exceptional. By 1880, St. Paul would have five thousand *fewer* residents than Minneapolis but also three more brothels than Minneapolis and sixty-six more saloons.[172]

It was with great difficulty that the police patrolled the city.

"Panoramic View of Lowertown in St. Paul from Rosabel Street," 1870. *Hennepin County Library Digital Collections.*

Steamboats at the Lower Levee, 1870. *Hennepin County Library Digital Collections.*

For the good reason that St. Paul abounded in unpaved, half-lit streets, walking at night was dangerous, and the policemen, especially those in the First and Second Wards, did all they could to maintain their "beats." The thugs and crooks outnumbered them three to one on every occasion of conflict, and of all desperate men, the gang of thieves and cutthroats infesting St. Paul during the early seventies was the worst. It included characters known to "rogues galleries" all over the Union.

This was just the backdrop. "Highway robbery and immorality were… not the worst features of the times, [compared to] a succession of murders, committed by citizens during the fall of 1874."[173] By that year, the total number of St. Paulites had risen to about thirty thousand. This autumn would go down in St. Paul Police history as the "Bloody Fall."[174] It began in actual fact in late summer with an "intentional and deliberate" murder.[175]

19

LAMB TO THE SLAUGHTER

I t was close to midnight on Monday, August 3, when Mike Kelly appeared at Ramsey County Jail. He told the sheriff's deputy that he had fought with his neighbor, Barney Lamb, and thought that he may have killed him. Sheriff John Grace had Kelly put in a cell, and then he went to the scene of the crime, at the back of Rice Street.

Barney Lamb, an expressman, had fallen where he was struck, in the Kellys' yard, but he had been carried into his own house, where he died before Sheriff Grace's arrival. He had been covered with a mosquito bar (netting to protect sleepers from mosquitos). Lamb had been stabbed five times in the chest and abdomen and once in the head. He had eight wounds, as the sword had gone clear through his body in some places. "The corpse presented a ghastly appearance, and a great deal of excitement existed in the neighborhood."[176]

The story that emerged by the next day was that, around 11:00 that night, Lamb had brought his tin pail with an attached rope to the Kellys' yard to draw water from the well. Mr. Kelly came out of the house and told him to leave. The men argued, and Lamb hit Kelly over the head with the pail. Kelly ran back into his house and returned with a short sword with an eighteen-inch blade. He stabbed Lamb over and over as Lamb fell to the ground.

BARNEY LAMB "HA[D] ALWAYS borne the reputation of a quiet, peaceable man." Kelly, however, was "described as a man of violent temper, and quarrelsome, especially when under the influence of liquor."[177] He had often appeared in the police court and had served short sentences in jail. The Kelly and Lamb families were close neighbors, and the Lambs were in the habit of drawing water from the well in the Kellys' yard. They had "for some time past been the best of friends, often assisting eachother [sic]."[178]

At some point in the days prior to the murder, Mrs. Lamb had told her husband that Mrs. Kelly had accused her of "keeping a house of ill-fame." On Sunday, Mr. Kelly brought his wife to the Lambs' house to "settle up." Instead, "words ensued between the two women, among which Mrs. Lamb made some taunting remark concerning Mrs. Kelly's working over the wash tub, to which Mrs. Kelly retorted that it was better than getting drunk as she did." Mr. Lamb kicked the Kellys out of his house, and Mr. Kelly forbade him to return to the well, "with dire threats if he did."[179] At the inquest on Tuesday morning, Mrs. Kelly said that Lamb kicked and bit her during the quarrel at his house.

Mr. Kelly's defense team consisted of Willis A. Gorman, now St. Paul City Attorney, and William W. Erwin. Mr. Erwin was a recent Ramsey County Attorney who had spent his time in office fighting corruption in local government, and he lost re-election after one term. Now, he was a rising star in criminal defense who would come to earn international acclaim for his rigorous advocacy for clients facing the death penalty.

At Mr. Kelly's trial in 1875, Gorman and Erwin argued that he had acted in self-defense. The jury was torn: ten stood for manslaughter, two for murder in the first degree. At Kelly's second trial, in May, the jury agreed on first-degree murder, and he was sentenced to life in prison. Mike Kelly had four children. Barney Lamb had five children. Now, nine children would grow up without a father in the home.

In 1888, Mike Kelly received a pardon. After all those years, he finally told the truth: it had been his wife who committed the murder. He had taken the blame for it to protect her.[180]

20

THE MURDER OF ULRICKA LICK

I went away a little after seven o'clock in the evening....I came [back] *to my house....My wife was leaning on my arm, we went into the kitchen which is separated from the main building; I started a little fire and my wife took off her new clothes and put on a linen coat belonging to one of the boys; she wanted to make a pan of dough to bake bread next morning; after she got through we were about leaving the kitchen when my wife said she was afraid for she thought she saw someone at the window looking in; she took up her clothes on her arm and left the kitchen....I walked up to the steps of my house and saw George Laudenschlaeger sitting on a pile of boards; Mrs. Rapp sat next to him and her husband, Frank Rapp, sat on the other side of this pile; this was on the west side of the house; my wife supposed it was one of her sons named Theodore who is after some girl, and called out "Theodore!"*

As she said this, Laudenschlaeger struck her right on the head; I saw the blood; I cannot tell what the weapon was, it was either an axe or a hammer; I heard the blow distinctly; I think I heard two blows; at the same time my wife was struck; Rapp caught me by the back of the neck; he had either a piece of iron or hard wood in his hand; I then fell down.

It was 10:00 a.m. on November 2, 1874, and Joseph Lick, a thirty-seven-year-old teamster, was giving his deposition to Christopher D. O'Brien, the Ramsey County Attorney, and Dr. Peter Garbrielson, the coroner. Mr.

Lick lay in bed, with his head and wrist in bandages, his face sliced with wounds. Although he was alert enough to tell his story, Lick was at high risk of profound health complications from inflammation, and he was attended by multiple doctors.

He showed O'Brien and Gabrielson a torn handkerchief.

> *This handkerchief was not cut as it is now when I put it on; when I was down Mrs. Rapp cut me in the face several times with a knife. She then felt for my throat and she and Rapp tried to get their hands* [underneath] *my throat, but could not on account of the handkerchief; Mrs. Rapp in attempting to cut my throat cut the handkerchief; Laudenschlaeger attempted to pull me into the little creek by my hair; and Mrs. Rapp cut my right wrist with the knife; at this time I had grappled Rapp with my right hand and it was at this time Mrs. Rapp cut my wrist; I was then lying on the ground and Laudenschlaeger twisted my face round into the sand and water and jumped with his full weight on the back of my neck and pressed my face down into the sand; a cow that was in Landenschlaeger's stable commenced coughing and he then let me go and jumped over the fence into his own yard; Rapp and his wife still continued to hold me; then I heard the noise of somebody on my steps and the door opening and they went away. None of these parties had boots or shoes on them; I had my senses until after they left me....You can ask my wife, she will tell you.*

Journalists, policemen and neighbors were in and out of the house the rest of the day. Joseph Lick asked constantly about his wife's condition. He begged to have her brought in to him so that he could see for himself how she was doing.

No one told him yet, not while his nerves were in such a weak state: His wife, Ulricka, lay in the entryway to the house, "her head shattered and streams of blood diverging in every direction from her head, so that you could scarcely pass the body either in going in or leaving the house without stepping in it." Someone had thrown a blanket over the body. A "pool of [her] blood on the outside and near the sidewalk leading to the house…was surrounded by a large crowd…who seemed to be attracted to the spot like a parcel of carrion crows."[181]

The murder weapon was as yet unidentified. Amateur detectives pawed through the boards and lumber in the yard of the Lick's Tenth Street house, near St. Peter Street.

The feud between the Licks and the Rapps had been going on for some time. Ulricka Lick had brought the property into her marriage. She had owned it with her first husband, Mr. Hayes, who died in a construction accident a few years earlier. About a year before her murder, she married Joseph Lick, a widower with six children. Ulricka had five children of her own. Together, Mr. and Mrs. Lick had twins, but they died within an hour of birth, three days after the Licks' marriage. The couple rallied and built a new house together, where they lived with all of their children.

The Licks did not need the entire lot for their own use, so they rented a section of it for twenty-five dollars per annum to Francis and Sophia Rapp, the brother-in-law and the sister of the Licks' neighbor, George Laudenschlaeger. Before her marriage to Mr. Lick, the widowed Mrs. Hayes had received frequent marriage proposals from Laudenschlaeger, with Mrs. Rapp's support. Since the wedding, Mrs. Rapp had threatened to kill Mrs. Lick and once came to the Licks' home with a knife, saying that she would slit Mrs. Lick's throat. As for the men, Laudenschlaeger (who married another woman) and Mr. Rapp quarreled with Mr. Lick over property disputes. On more than one occasion, the Rapps and Licks had bickered so intensely that the police had had to intervene to stop them from "inflicting serious injuries on each other." There were two fires on the property that year.

Mr. and Mrs. Lick "are represented to have been peaceable, hardworking people," while the Rapps, especially Mrs. Rapp, were "noted for extremely quarrelsome dispositions."[182]

The Rapps and Laudenschlaeger were charged with murder. Joseph Lick's death was reported, but erroneously. He showed signs of recovery. Meanwhile, Francis Rapp's brother Valentine found a bottle of poisoned whiskey in Francis's house, which the police theorized was intended for the Licks.

Francis Rapp insisted that the bottle of poisoned whiskey had been prepared by his sister and her brother to kill him. His credibility was somewhat damaged by the fact that he had begun to show symptoms of severe mental illness. His apparent decline was dramatic, and he was not expected to recover during his lifetime. A Catholic priest performed last rites for him. Mr. Rapp either recovered his senses or was posturing, because he was lucid enough to be tried for murder in April of the following year.

Mr. Erwin appeared for the defense, along with Isaac Heard, and yet the three defendants didn't stand a chance. There was the history of the feud between the families and damning scene-of-crime evidence: the police had observed bloody tracks from the Licks' house to Laudenschlaeger's house, which seemed to have been made by a person wearing soft slippers. The jury convicted Mr. Rapp of murder in the first degree." He was sentenced to life in prison. Eleven jurors wanted him hanged, but the lone holdout saved him. The other two were also convicted. Mr. Erwin succeeded in getting a second trial for Mrs. Rapp, this time with a change of venue in Minneapolis. She was again found guilty and sentenced to life in prison, "or until pardoned out." Laudenschlaeger alone was sentenced to death, as he was alleged to have been the one to deal the death blows to Mrs. Lick. Judge Hascal R. Brill allowed Laudenschlaeger the mercy of being taken out of jail for a day to go home and view the body of his child, who had died the day before. While there, Laudenschlaeger verbally abused his wife "with revilings and cursings."[183]

Like the Kelly-Lamb murder, this crime had a bizarre coda. In November, Joseph Lick was arrested for the murder of his newborn twins. Theodore Hayes, his eldest stepchild, now an adult, accused him of drowning them in a basin of water thirty minutes after their birth. He also said that his stepfather was his mother's real killer.

According to the stepson, he and his minor siblings were turned out of the house after the death of their mother, which would have been sufficient to stimulate acrimony. In addition to that, Theodore and Lick were at that time ensnared in an ugly inheritance dispute. Mrs. Lick, disposing of her property as she saw fit, had willed it to her second husband. It was Theodore's contention that his father had never intended to will it to his mother in the first place and that it should have come directly to the Hayes children. He alleged malfeasance on the part of the notary public who had certified Mr. Hayes's will. Theodore put forth other reasons why the property should not go to his stepfather, such as the fact that he was not a U.S. citizen.

The charges for the murder of the twins were dropped, but there were two more lawsuits over the property. In both cases, prior to a crucial court appearance, somebody burned down the Licks' house, where he was still living with his own children. After the second fire, in 1878, one of his children needed hospitalization. The fires would have been in Theodore's favor: if he won his suit, then he would have to pay his stepfather for the cost of improvements to the property. If the improvements were destroyed prior to the court's ruling, he would not have to pay. The suspicions that Theodore had expressed about his stepfather could have contributed to the fact that Laudenschlaeger was no longer under sentence of death.

Then George Hermon came home. He was a St. Paulite who had left for New York on November 2, 1874, the day after Ulricka Lick was murdered.

He had been unaware of the case until he read about it more recently, owing to newspaper coverage of the inheritance squabble. It jogged his memory. He had seen something, heard something, the day before he left, that had meant nothing at the time. In his January 1879 affidavit, Hermon stated that he had been walking past the Lick property in the late evening and heard Joseph Lick shouting at his wife and threatening her.

In February 1881, the state prison committee recommended that the legislature authorize the retrials of Laudenschlaeger and the Rapps. The legislature did not comply, but Governor Lucius F. Hubbard commuted their sentences, and they were released in October 1886. The three of them went to Laudenschlaeger's small house on Tenth Street, "in the shadow of the more pretentious residence of Lick."[184] At that time, Joseph Lick was a rich man, his wealth estimated at $500,000. He was also tight-fisted and tried to get away with cutting financial corners. He periodically had fines assessed against his property. Soon after his neighbors were released from prison, Judge Henry W. Cory fined him $50 for larceny. Lick had stolen wood from a lumberyard on Dayton's Bluff for a house he was building in the neighborhood. He fought the sentence, and the judge doubled it to $100.

After just a few days at home, Mr. Rapp, who was "weak in mind and body," told his family that he was going to visit a friend on West Seventh Street, near the Short Line crossing. He never got there.[185] At the time of his disappearance, he was waiting to give testimony to exonerate the former prison warden, implicating the current one. Some suspected a conspiracy; more likely, he was just a sad, broken man who wandered away.

21
URBAN ASSASSINATION

Contrary to ethnic stereotypes, the Irish-born Patrick O'Connor was a staid teetotaler, a member of the Father Mathew Temperance Society. He was a thirty-seven-year-old man of "quiet, inoffensive habits," with a small family.[186] His wife was pregnant with their second child, whose birth was just around the corner. It must have been a shock to those who knew O'Connor when he was arrested for assault on Tuesday, November 10, 1894. He appeared in police court the next day.

On Monday the ninth, O'Connor, the foreman for the contractor Isaac W. Elliott, had fired John Rose for incompetency. John's two brothers also worked there, but they kept their jobs. John left the construction site at Fourth and Sibley Streets and went drinking. He came back and started taunting and threatening O'Connor. Elliott got between them and told John to leave. Instead, John shoved him aside and charged at O'Connor, who was standing by an excavation pit. In fear of being thrown down into it, he raised the pickaxe that he'd been holding in his hand and struck John with the handle, knocking him backward. Rose fell, sustaining a wound to his scalp, but he jumped up again. He stormed off to the police court, and that was how O'Connor ended up there on Wednesday.

The court dismissed the charges, as O'Connor had acted in self-defense. As John Rose and his brothers left the courtroom, where they had come to give evidence against O'Connor, they threatened not only O'Connor but also Mr. Elliott and the judge.

Around 4:30 that afternoon, O'Connor was busy fixing a temporary fence around the excavation site. John Rose approached him from the south side of Fourth Street, carrying a double-barreled shotgun. He paused when he got to within twenty or thirty feet of his target. He leveled the gun and exclaimed, "Now, you s[on] of a b[itch], I'll be even with you!"[187]

A second before he spoke, an onlooker saw him and shouted a warning to O'Connor. To protect himself, O'Connor held up two light boards nailed together, which he had been using to make the fence. He put them in front of his face, but the shot passed through the boards. The wood absorbed some of the charge, but not enough.

John Rose, gun in hand, ran down Fourth Street, with a crowd chasing behind him. A couple of hackmen joined the hunt. A police officer jumped into one of the hacks. Rose turned down a side street and took it to Seventh. On the corner of Seventh and Jackson, Officer Putzier caught and arrested him. The crowd shouted, "Lynch him! Lynch him!" Putzier's colleagues had to draw their clubs to intimidate the mob into submission, and they brought the killer to jail.

O'Connor could walk, until he couldn't. He grew faint, and he was brought to Dr. Murphy's office on Jackson Street. Dr. Waite, Murphy's colleague, examined his injuries. O'Connor looked as if he had taken a blow from a blunt object on the left side of his face. He also had wounds all over his eye, ear, neck and cheek. In the doctors' opinion, he had taken at least thirty shots to his face, and some of them entered his optic nerve, rupturing the eye.

The doctors dressed O'Connor's wounds and then brought him to his home. Mrs. O'Connor had not been told of the shooting, and when she saw her husband's face, "Her Cries and Groans Were Agonizing." The doctors got her to understand that their patient should not be disturbed in this way. She quieted down. O'Connor's sister, who had heard the news, came into the house, "and her screams rang out clear and wild, again exciting the unfortunate wife to such a degree that Dr. Waite…had to use force to get both of them out of the room." He did all he could to keep O'Connor comfortable through the night. He did such a good job of this that there was some hope, which he did not encourage, that the victim would live.

In the morning, a mob gathered at the county jail. It would have been standard practice to have put Rose in city lockup, but the authorities had decided that the county facilities would be easier to defend from lynching attempts. Another crowd, with similar motives, swarmed around City Hall, waiting for Rose to be taken to a preliminary examination. The county attorney postponed it.

Patrick O'Connor died. At the news of his death, the public's agitation rose.

> *Groups of men could be seen talking over the matter on street corners and in*
> *saloons, and an evident intention was manifested that the perpetrator of the*
> *bloody deed should have swift and sharp justice dealt out to him, and that*
> *no hawkish* [sic] *sensibility should restrain the arm of justice from dealing*
> *out this punishment.*[188]

The county was able to protect Rose from lynching, and he was tried for first-degree murder. His attorneys presented an insanity defense, but the jury convicted him of murder in the first degree. Wednesday, June 2, 1875, saw a crowded Ramsey County courthouse. Spectators had come to watch the show, as two judges between them handed down four life sentences: Judge Brill gave the first one to Frank Rapp, and Judge Orlando Simons gave the next three to Mike Kelly, John Rose and then to Fred Hifler, who had been convicted of child sexual assault. Rose received a pardon in 1897, after twenty-three years in prison.

HAVING REVIEWED THE ENTIRE history of the St. Paul crime annals up to 1900, the reporter Muller was confident that the record of the mid-1870s "is but a glimpse into a past which can never repeat itself; a skeleton dragged out of a city closet."[189]

NOTES

Prologue

1. Hrapsky, "'Keep St. Paul Boring'."

Chapter 1

2. *Saint Paul Globe*, "Building Up of Fort Snelling"; legally, they were squatters, but they did not see themselves that way.
3. Beyond the settlers' whiskey-selling, both Plympton and others would suggest additional motives for him wanting them gone, none of which are sufficient: He said that they used too much lumber; he begrudged their livestock grazing on the parade ground; and his enemies claimed that he was running a real estate grift that would profit by the settlers' removal. The fact is that Plympton, his officers, and his superiors were in general agreement that whiskey sellers posed a danger to the fort and the region, and this was the basis for the War Department authorizing removal; Williams, *History of Saint Paul*, 58–59; Most of the history of Fort Snelling is undisputed. However, the account which follows, in which the Selkirk settlement is the reason for the establishment of Fort Snelling, may be an element of Minnesota state mythos. Minnesotan historians tend to subscribe to this narrative, but the Iowan historian Marcus L. Hansen does not mention it in his discussion of the factors that led the federal government to desire a military outpost in the region. Hansen, *Old Fort Snelling*.

4. Taliaferro, *Auto-biography of Major Taliaferro*, 216.

5. Ibid., 210.

6. Treaties Matter, "1837 Land Cession Treaties with the Ojibwe & Dakota."

7. Taliaferro, *Auto-biography of Major Taliaferro*, 232.

8. Ibid., 232–33.

Chapter 2

9. Taliaferro, *Auto-biography of Major Taliaferro*, 72.

10. Taliaferro, *Auto-biography of Major Taliaferro*, 71; Neill and Williams, *History of Ramsey County*, 182, 302.

11. Williams, *History of Saint Paul*, 73.

12. Ibid., 90.

13. Common among frontiersmen, as there were few unmarried white women there at the time.

14. Not to be confused with "the bottom of the river." A "river bottom" is the strip of rich, damp soil along the edge of a riverbank.

15. Williams, 91.

16. *Taliaferro Journal*, September 15, 1939, quoted in Williams, *History of Saint Paul*, 91.

17. Williams, *History of Saint Paul*, 91.

18. Brueggemann, *Minnesota's Oldest Murder Mystery*, 170.

19. *Brown's Casebook*, 252, quoted in Brueggemann, *Minnesota's Oldest Murder Mystery*, 79.

20. Ibid.

21. On June 11, 2007, the historian Gary Brueggemann interviewed clerical staff at the Crawford County Courthouse, as Prairie du Chien is located in Crawford County. He learned that they have nothing on Edward Phelan. At some point in the intervening 167 years, the Phelan case record had gone missing (Brueggemann, *Minnesota's Oldest Murder Mystery*).

22. Ibid.

23. Williams, *History of Saint Paul*, 92–3.

24. Ibid., 92.

25. Ibid., 93.

Chapter 3

26. Dr. Emerson, a slaveholder, was an utterly inconsequential man, aside from the fact that one of the enslaved people in his "possession," Dred Scott, would famously fight a legal battle for his freedom. Scott's wife, Harriet Robinson, had come to Fort Snelling in Agent Taliaferro's captivity. Taliaferro married them when he was justice of the peace and then sold Mrs. Scott to Emerson so that the couple could stay together. In Taliaferro's warped version of morality, this seemed the right thing to do, as opposed to buying Dred Scott and freeing them both. The Scotts would later use their legal marriage as part of their evidence in court for why they should be free, as enslaved people were usually denied the right of legal marriage.
27. Williams, *History of Saint Paul*, 79–80.
28. Ibid., 80.
29. Ibid., 81.
30. Taliaferro, *Auto-biography of Major Taliaferro*, 226; ; quoted in Hansen, *Old Fort Snelling*, 194.
31. Ibid., 93.
32. Ibid.
33. Ibid., 94.
34. Ibid., 100.
35. DeCarlo, *Fort Snelling at Bdote*, 40.
36. Larpenteur, "Tales of the Days When St. Paul Was Nothing."
37. Ibid.
38. Williams, *History of Saint Paul*, 108.

Chapter 4

39. Ibid., 210.
40. Ibid., 211.
41. Ibid.
42. Ibid., 211–12.
43. Ibid., 228.
44. Ibid., 211.
45. Ibid., 234.
46. *Minnesota Pioneer*, "Absentee Office Holders."

47. Williams, *History of Minnesota*, 285.
48. Newson, *Pen Pictures of St. Paul, Minnesota*, 335, 259.

Chapter 5

49. Williams, *History of Minnesota*, 236.
50. Newson, *Pen Pictures of St. Paul, Minnesota*, 87.
51. Williams, *History of Minnesota*, 258.
52. Newson, *Pen Pictures of St. Paul, Minnesota*, 172.
53. Ibid., 213.
54. Williams, *History of Minnesota*, 327.
55. Ibid., 331.

Chapter 6

56. Also translated as "His Red Nation," "His Scarlet People" and "His Red People."
57. There are as many versions of this story as there are tellers, but this seems to have been the most plausible account.
58. Larpenteur, "Tales of the Days When St. Paul Was Nothing."
59. Williams, *History of Minnesota*, 284.
60. Folwell, *History of Minnesota*, Vol. 1., 254.
61. Ibid., 255.
62. Ibid., 266.
63. DeCarlo, *Fort Snelling at Bdote*, 43.
64. Folwell, *History of Minnesota*, Vol. 1, 270–71.
65. Ibid., 283.
66. DeCarlo, *Fort Snelling at Bdote*, 44.
67. Ibid., 286.
68. Ibid., 287.

Chapter 7

69. Neill and Williams, *History of Ramsey County*, 124.
70. Larpenteur, "Tales of the Days When St. Paul Was Nothing."

71. Williams, *History of Minnesota*, 344.

72. Ibid., 346.

73. *Minnesota Pioneer*, "Foul Murder."

74. Newson, *Pen Pictures of St. Paul, Minnesota*, 388.

75. Ibid., 337.

76. Ibid., 448.

77. Ibid.

78. Ibid., 394.

79. Ibid., 448.

80. Ibid., 321.

Chapter 8

81. Neill and Williams, *History of Ramsey County*, 218.

82. Newson, *Pen Pictures*, 570.

83. Neill and Williams, *History of Ramsey County*, 319.

84. Doran, *History of the Saint Paul Police Department*.

85. Williams, *History of Minnesota*, 364.

86. Ibid.

87. Newson, *Pen Pictures of St. Paul, Minnesota*, 638.

88. Williams, *History of Saint Paul*, 369.

89. *Weekly Minnesotian*, "City. Brutal Murder at the 'Cave'."

90. Ibid.

91. Newson, *Pen Pictures of St. Paul, Minnesota*, 640.

Chapter 9

92. Williams, *History of Saint Paul*, 376.

93. Ibid., 376–77.

94. Newson, *Pen Pictures of St. Paul, Minnesota*, 666.

95. Ibid., 666.

96. Ibid.

97. Williams, *History of Saint Paul*, 379.

98. Ibid., 380.

99. Newson, *Pen Pictures of St. Paul, Minnesota*, 666.

100. Williams, *History of Saint Paul*, 380.

101. Ibid.

102. *Stillwater Messenger*, "Most Ruffianly Assault by Governor Gorman."

103. *Weekly Minnesotian*, "Financial Crisis—No Cause for Alarm."

104. Williams, *History of Saint Paul*, 381.

105. Newson, *Pen Pictures of St. Paul, Minnesota*, 698.

106. Neill and Williams, *History of Ramsey County*, 130.

107. Williams, *History of Saint Paul*, 358.

108. Newson, *Pen Pictures of St. Paul, Minnesota*, 323.

109. Ibid., 325.

110. Newson, *Pen Pictures of St. Paul, Minnesota*, 323.

111. Ibid., 324.

Chapter 10

112. Ibid.

113. Ibid.

114. *Pioneer and Democrat*, May 25, 1859, quoted in Cecil, "Justice in Heaven," 350–63, 357.

115. Ibid.

116. Cecil, "Justice in Heaven," 357.

117. Trenerry, *Murder in Minnesota*, 32–33.

118. *Pioneer and Democrat*, "Sentence of Mrs. Bilansky."

119. *Pioneer and Democrat*, January 10, 1860, quoted in Cecil, "Justice in Heaven, 360.

120. Cecil, "Justice in Heaven," 361.

121. *Pioneer and Democrat*, "Bilansky Murder."

122. Ibid.

123. *Pioneer and Democrat*, March 24, 1860, quoted in Trenerry, *Murder in Minnesota*, 41.

124. Ibid.

125. *Pioneer and Democrat*, "Bilansky Murder."

126. *Stillwater Messenger*, "Mrs. Bilansky Strangled."

Chapter 11

127. Williams, *History of Saint Paul*, 392.

Chapter 12

128. Doran, *History of the Saint Paul Police Department.*
129. Ibid.

Chapter 13

130. *St. Paul Daily Press*, "Who Is to Blame!"
131. Diedrich, "Chief Hole-in-the-Day," 195.
132. Folwell, *History of Minnesota*, Vol. 2, 396.
133. Ibid., 398.
134. Ibid., 238.
135. Diedrich, "Chief Hole-in-the-Day," 193.
136. Newson, "Indian Affairs Ten, Fifteen and Thirty Miles from St. Paul."
137. Folwell, *History of Minnesota*, Vol. 2, 255.
138. Ibid., 127.
139. DeCarlo, *Fort Snelling at Bdote*, 57.
140. *Weekly Pioneer and Democrat*, "Execution of the Condemned Indians."
141. DeCarlo, *History of Fort Snelling at Bdote*, 54.
142. Folwell, *History of Minnesota*, Vol. 2, 259.
143. Brown, "In 1865, Two Dakota Leaders Meet a Gruesome End."
144. *Mankato Union*, "Shakopee and Medicine Bottle."
145. *Mankato Union*. "Indian Execution."
146. Folwell, *History of Minnesota*, Vol. 2, 345.
147. Newson, *Pen Pictures*, 125.

Chapter 14

148. *Saint Paul Press*, "Steamboat Explosion."
149. Ibid.
150. Williams, *History of Minnesota*, 416.

Chapter 15

151. *Weekly Pioneer and Democrat*, "Horrible Tragedy!"

152. *Saint Paul Press*, "Murder and Suicide."
153. *Weekly Pioneer and Democrat*, "Horrible Tragedy!"
154. Ibid.

Chapter 16

155. Williams, *History of Saint Paul*, 417.
156. Ibid., 419.
157. *Saint Paul Press*, "Indian War. Major Brackett's Battalion Ordered to Sioux City."
158. *Saint Paul Press*, "Ghastly Head."
159. *Saint Paul Press*, "Police Court."
160. Williams, *History of Saint Paul*, 420.
161. Ibid., 424–25.
162. *St. Paul Daily Globe*, "Two Wee Small Mice."
163. *St. Paul City Council Proceedings, 1863–1883*, 86–87, quoted in Nelson, "Early Days of the State Reform School."

Chapter 17

164. *Minneapolis Tribune*, "Coincidence: Death of Senator C.K. Davis Recalls a Tragedy of 32 Years Ago."
165. *Dodge County Republican*, "The West."
166. *St. Cloud Journal*, "Startling Charge."
167. *Sauk Centre Herald*, "Van Solen Case."
168. *Saint Paul Globe*, "Where Davis Won Fame."
169. *St. Cloud Journal*, "Acquittal of Van Solen."

Chapter 18

170. Holcombe, "Leading Events in the History of St. Paul from the Year 1854," 68–112.
171. Mead and Muller, *History of the Police and Fire Departments of the Twin Cities*, Vol. 2, 55.

172. Best, "Keeping the Peace in St. Paul," 242.
173. Ibid.
174. Doran, *History of the Saint Paul Police Department.*
175. *Minneapolis Daily Tribune*, "The Murder."

Chapter 19

176. *Mower County Transcript*, "Another Murder."
177. Ibid.
178. *Waseca Weekly News*, "Man Murdered."
179. Ibid.
180. *St. Paul Daily Globe*, "'Lifer' Set Free."

Chapter 20

181. *Anti-Monopolist*, "Bloody Murder."
182. Ibid.
183. *St. Cloud Journal*, "Minnesota News."
184. *St. Paul Daily Globe*, "Joseph Lick."
185. *St. Paul Daily Press*, "Is There a Plot In It?"

Chapter 21

186. *Anti-Monopolist*, "Human Life Cheap."
187. Ibid.
188. Ibid.
189. Mead and Muller, *History of the Police and Fire Departments of the Twin Cities*, Vol. 2, 55..

BIBLIOGRAPHY

Anti-Monopolist (St. Paul, MN). "Bloody Murder. A Man and Wife
    Assaulted. The Wife Instantly Killed. Two Men and a Woman
    the Murderers." November 5, 1874. Chronicling America:
    Historic American Newspapers, Library of Congress. https://
    chroniclingamerica.loc.gov.
———. "Human Life Cheap. Cold Blooded Murder in St. Paul."
    November 12, 1874. Chronicling America: Historic American
    Newspapers, Library of Congress. https://chroniclingamerica.loc.gov.
Best, Joel. "Keeping the Peace in St. Paul: CRIME, VICE, and POLICE
    WORK, 1869-74." *Minnesota History* (Summer 1981): 240–48.
Brown, Curt. "In 1865, Two Dakota Leaders Meet a Gruesome End." *Star
    Tribune*, November 8, 2015.
Brueggemann, Gary. *Minnesota's Oldest Murder Mystery: The Case of Edward
    Phalen: St. Paul's Unsaintly Pioneer.* St. Paul, MN: Beaver's Pond Press,
    2012.
Cecil, Matthew. "Justice in Heaven: The Trial and Execution of Ann
    Bilansky." *Minnesota History* (Winter 1997–98): 350–63.
DeCarlo, Peter. *Fort Snelling at Bdote.* St. Paul, MN: Minnesota Historical
    Society Press, 2016.
Diedrich, Mark. "Chief Hole-in-the-Day and the 1862 Chippewa
    Disturbance: A Reappraisal." *Minnesota History* (Spring 1987): 193–203.
Dodge County (MN) Republican. "The West." September 28, 1867. Minnesota
    Digital Newspaper Hub, Minnesota Historical Society. https://
    newspapers.mnhs.org.

Doran, Maurice E. *History of the Saint Paul Police Department*. St. Paul, MN: Saint Paul Police Historical Society, 1912. https://www.spphs.org.

Farber, Zac. "The Moral Arc of Indian Agent Lawrence Taliaferro." *Minnesota Lawyer* (January 3, 2019). https://minnlawyer.com.

Folwell, William Watts. *A History of Minnesota*. Vol. 1. St. Paul: Minnesota Historical Press, 1922.

———. *A History of Minnesota*. Vol. 2. St. Paul: Minnesota Historical Society Press, 1924.

Hansen, Marcus Lee. *Old Fort Snelling, 1819–1858*. Iowa City, State Historical Society of Iowa, 1918.

Holcombe, Return I. "Leading Events in the History of St. Paul from the Year 1854." In *History of St. Paul, Minn*, edited by C.C. Andrews, 68–112. Syracuse, NY: D. Mason & Company, 1890.

Hrapsky, Chris. "'Keep St. Paul Boring' Slogan Born Out of Love." May 19, 2017. Kare11. https://www.kare11.com.

Josiah Snelling Papers, 1779–1828. M683. Manuscript Collection on microfilm. Minnesota Historical Society, St. Paul.

Larpenteur, A.L. "Tales of the Days When St. Paul Was Nothing but an Indian Community." *Saint Paul Globe*, May 22, 1904. Minnesota Digital Newspaper Hub, Minnesota Historical Society. https://newspapers.mnhs.org.

Mankato (MN) Union. "Indian Execution: Medicine Bottle and Shakopee Executed Friday Last, Nov. 12th. Extracts from the St. Paul Press of Nov. 12." November 17, 1865. Minnesota Digital Newspaper Hub, Minnesota Historical Society. https://newspapers.mnhs.org.

———. "Shakopee and Medicine Bottle: How They Received the Order for Execution." November 17, 1865. Minnesota Digital Newspaper Hub.

Mead, Frank J., and Alix J. Muller. *History of the Police and Fire Departments of the Twin Cities: Their Origin in Early Village Days and Progress to 1900. Historical and Biographical*. Vol. 2. Minneapolis, MN: American Land & Title Register Association, 1899.

Minneapolis Daily Tribune. "The Murder." August 5, 1874. Minnesota Digital Newspaper Hub, Minnesota Historical Society. https://newspapers.mnhs.org.

Minneapolis Tribune. "Coincidence: Death of Senator C. K. Davis Recalls a Tragedy of 32 Years Ago. Dr. Van Solen, Whom He Defended, Also a Victim of Blood Poisoning. Both Had the Peculiar Red Mark, One on the Toe, the Other on the Finger." December 6, 1900. Minnesota Digital Newspaper Hub, Minnesota Historical Society. https://newspapers.mnhs.org.

Minnesota Historical Society. https://newspapers.mnhs.org.

Minnesota Pioneer (St. Paul, MN). "Absentee Office Holders." January 16, 1851. Chronicling America: Historic American Newspapers, Library of Congress. https://chroniclingamerica.loc.gov.

———. "Foul Murder." January 5, 1854. Chronicling America: Historic American Newspapers, Library of Congress. https://chroniclingamerica.loc.gov.

Mower County Transcript (Lansing, MN). "Another Murder." August 6, 1874. Minnesota Digital Newspaper Hub, Minnesota Historical Society. https://newspapers.mnhs.org.

Neill, Edward D., and Fletcher Williams. *History of Ramsey County and the City of St. Paul, Including the Explorers and Pioneers of Minnesota by Rev. Edward D. Neill, and Outlines of the History of Minnesota, by Fletcher Williams.* Minneapolis, MN: North Star Publishing Company, 1881.

Nelson, Paul D. "Early Days of the State Reform School." *Minnesota History* (Winter 2012–13): 132–43. http://collections.mnhs.org.

———. "St. Paul City Hall and Ramsey County Courthouse." March 9, 2022. *MNopedia*. https://www.mnopedia.org/structure/st-paul-city-hall-and-ramsey-county-courthouse

Newson, Thomas M. "Indian Affairs Ten, Fifteen and Thirty Miles from St. Paul." *Saint Paul Daily Press*, August 30, 1862. Minnesota Digital Newspaper Hub, Minnesota Historical Society. https://newspapers.mnhs.org.

———. *Pen Pictures of St. Paul, Minnesota, and Biographical Sketches of Old Settlers, From the Earliest Settlement of the City, Up to and Including the Year 1857.* St. Paul: Minnesota Historical Society Press, 1884.

Pioneer and Democrat (St. Paul, MN). "The Bilansky Murder." March 30, 1860. Chronicling America: Historic American Newspapers, Library of Congress. https://chroniclingamerica.loc.gov.

———. "The Sentence of Mrs. Bilansky." December 3, 1859. Chronicling America: Historic American Newspapers, Library of Congress. https://chroniclingamerica.loc.gov.

Saint Paul Globe. "The Building Up of Fort Snelling." July 3, 1904. Minnesota Digital Newspaper Hub, Minnesota Historical Society. https://newspapers.mnhs.org.

———. "Where Davis Won Fame." July 19, 1903. Chronicling America: Historic American Newspapers, Library of Congress. https://chroniclingamerica.loc.gov.

Saint Paul Press. "The Ghastly Head." May 25, 1865. Minnesota Digital Newspaper Hub, Minnesota Historical Society. https://newspapers.mnhs.org.

———. "The Indian War. Major Brackett's Battalion Ordered to Sioux City." April 1, 1865. Minnesota Digital Newspaper Hub, Minnesota Historical Society. https://newspapers.mnhs.org.

———. "Latest from the Frontier; Terribly Exciting News; Hanging of a Sioux Half-Breed by Mob Law. He Was Identified as one of the Murderers of the Jewett Family. Confession of the Murderer. Nine Sioux War Parties in the Neighborhood. Rev. Dr. Williamson, a Sioux Missionary, Driven from the City." May 5, 1865. Minnesota Digital Newspaper Hub, Minnesota Historical Society. https://newspapers. mnhs.org.

———. "Murder and Suicide: A Mother Kills Two of Her Children, and Cuts Her Own Throat in a Fit of Insanity. Another Child Badly Injured, but Still Alive. Horrible Spectacle at the Place of the Tragedy." December 23, 1864. Minnesota Digital Newspaper Hub, Minnesota Historical Society. https://newspapers.mnhs.org.

———. "Police Court." July 9, 1865. Minnesota Digital Newspaper Hub, Minnesota Historical Society. https://newspapers.mnhs.org.

———. "Steamboat Explosion. The John Rumsey Blown up and Sunk. Five Men Instantly Killed and One Supposed to Be Drowned. Still Another Missing. Nine Others Severely Injured. Names of the Killed and Wounded. Full Particulars of the Accident." November 5, 1864. Minnesota Digital Newspaper Hub, Minnesota Historical Society. https://newspapers.mnhs.org.

Saint Paul Weekly Minnesotian. "The Bilansky Poisoning Case—Second Inquest." March 19, 1859. Minnesota Digital Newspaper Hub, Minnesota Historical Society. https://newspapers.mnhs.org.

Sauk Centre (MN) Herald. "The Van Solen Case." October 24, 1867. Minnesota Digital Newspaper Hub, Minnesota Historical Society. https://newspapers.mnhs.org.

St. Cloud (MN) Journal. "The Acquittal of Van Solen." August 13, 1868. Chronicling America: Historic American Newspapers, Library of Congress. https://chroniclingamerica.loc.gov.

———. "Minnesota News." September 23, 1875. Chronicling America: Historic American Newspapers, Library of Congress. https:// chroniclingamerica.loc.gov.

———. "Startling Charge." September 26, 1867. Chronicling America: Historic American Newspapers, Library of Congress. https:// chroniclingamerica.loc.gov.

Stillwater (MN) Messenger. "Most Ruffianly Assault by Governor Gorman upon a Republican Member of the Compromise Committee." September 1, 1857. Minnesota Digital Newspaper Hub, Minnesota Historical Society. https://newspapers.mnhs.org.

———. "Mrs. Bilansky Strangled." March 27, 1860. Minnesota Digital Newspaper Hub, Minnesota Historical Society. https://newspapers.mnhs.org.

St. Paul Daily Globe. "Joseph Lick, a Half-Millionaire, Fined $50 in the Police Court." October 21, 1887. Chronicling America: Historic American Newspapers, Library of Congress. https://chroniclingamerica.loc.gov.

———. "A 'Lifer Set Free." April 9, 1888. Minnesota Digital Newspaper Hub, Minnesota Historical Society. https://newspapers.mnhs.org.

———. "Two Wee Small Mice." October 11, 1889. Chronicling America: Historic American Newspapers, Library of Congress. https://chroniclingamerica.loc.gov.

St. Paul Daily Press. "Is There a Plot In It? Recently Relieved Convicts Are Rapidly Getting Out of the Way." October 14, 1887. Chronicling America: Historic American Newspapers, Library of Congress. https://chroniclingamerica.loc.gov.

———. "Who Is to Blame!" September 11, 1862. Minnesota Digital Newspaper Hub, Minnesota Historical Society. https://newspapers.mnhs.org.

Taliaferro, Lawrence. *Auto-biography of Major Taliaferro.* St. Paul: Minnesota Historical Society, 1894

Treaties Matter. "1837 Land Cession Treaties with the Ojibwe & Dakota." https://treatiesmatter.org.

Trenerry, Walter N. *Murder in Minnesota: A Collection of True Cases.* St. Paul: Minnesota Historical Society Press, 1962.

United States Census Bureau. Minnesota. 1940. https://www2.census.gov.

Der Wanderer. "Der Kelly Mordprozek." April 24, 1875. https://chroniclingamerica.loc.gov.

———. "Der Lick Mordprozek." September 18, 1875. https://chroniclingamerica.loc.gov.

———. "Der Lick Mordprozek." April 10, 1875. https://chroniclingamerica.loc.gov.

———. "Gerichts Urtheile." June 5, 1875. https://chroniclingamerica.loc.gov.

Waseca (MN) Weekly News. "A Man Murdered." August 12, 1874. Minnesota Digital Newspaper Hub, Minnesota Historical Society. https://newspapers.mnhs.org.

Weekly Minnesotian (St. Paul, MN). "The City. Brutal Murder at the 'Cave.'" May 16, 1857. Chronicling America: Historic American Newspapers, Library of Congress. https://chroniclingamerica.loc.gov.

———. "The Financial Crisis—No Cause for Alarm." Minnesota Digital Newspaper Hub, Minnesota Historical Society. https://newspapers. mnhs.org.

Weekly Pioneer and Democrat (St. Paul, MN). "The Execution of the Condemned Indians." December 5, 1862. Chronicling America: Historic American Newspapers, Library of Congress. https:// chroniclingamerica.loc.gov.

———. "A Horrible Tragedy! A Triple Murder and Suicide! A Mother Kills Two of Her Children, Mortally Wounds a Third, and Then Takes Her Own Life. A Carnival of Crime!" November 30, 1864. Chronicling America: Historic American Newspapers, Library of Congress. https:// chroniclingamerica.loc.gov.

Williams, J. Fletcher. *A History of Saint Paul, and of the County of Ramsey, Minnesota*. St. Paul: Minnesota Historical Society Press, 1876.

Workers of the Writers' Project of the Work Projects Administration of the State of Minnesota. *Minneapolis: The Story of a City*. Minneapolis Department of Education/Minneapolis Board of Education, 1940.

INDEX

ABOUT THE AUTHOR

R on de Beaulieu came to St. Paul for college. She left for a year but couldn't stay away, and she came back to the area to go to grad school at the University of Minnesota. She now lives in Minneapolis, but still loves exploring St. Paul. Her new favorite spot there is Shadow Falls. Ron is also the author of *Minneapolis Murder & Mayhem*.